FLOWERCRAFTS

FLOWERCRAFTS

Practical inspirations for natural gifts,
country crafts and decorative displays

DEENA BEVERLEY

PHOTOGRAPHY BY MICHELLE GARRETT

LORENZ BOOKS

LONDON • NEW YORK • SYDNEY • BATH

For my mother,
who taught me to make
the ordinary extraordinary.
I miss you.

––––––––– ❧ –––––––––

This edition published in 1997 by Lorenz Books

Lorenz Books is an imprint of
Anness Publishing Limited
Hermes House
88-89 Blackfriars Road
London SE1 8HA

This edition published in Canada by Lorenz Books,
distributed by Raincoast Books Limited, Vancouver

ISBN 1 85967 374 0

A CIP catalogue entry for this book is available at the British Library.

Publisher: JOANNA LORENZ
Project Editor: JUDITH SIMONS
Designer: ANNIE MOSS
Mac Artist: JOHN FOWLER
Photographer: MICHELLE GARRETT
Stylist: DEENA BEVERLEY
Illustrator: KIM GLASS

Printed and bound in Singapore

1 3 5 7 9 10 8 6 4 2

CONTENTS

The Flowercraft Tradition 6

For Giving and Celebrating 60

The Still Room 20

For Pampering and Fragrancing 86

For Embellishing the Home 34

For Entertaining and Feasting 110

The
FLOWERCRAFT
TRADITION

TO SEE A WORLD IN A GRAIN OF SAND,
AND A HEAVEN IN A WILD FLOWER,
HOLD INFINITY IN THE PALM OF YOUR HAND,
AND ETERNITY IN AN HOUR.

(William Blake, 1757-1827)

ABOVE AND LEFT: *The impulse to capture and celebrate the fleeting beauty of freshly gathered flowers has inspired an ancient tradition of floral art and craft.*

INTRODUCTION

Flowers are potent symbols and have often played a central role in myths and legends; their poetical beauty continues to charm and inspire people of every culture. But they also have a much more tangible place in the flowercraft tradition, used in lotions and potions devised as beauty preparations and for medicinal purposes.

Flowers have been enjoyed in the home for centuries. The instinct to bring the colour, fragrance and life-enhancing qualities of fresh flowers and leaves indoors is basic to people all over the world. Many flowers have symbolic meaning or health-giving properties, which were greatly valued in the past and are beginning to be appreciated again today. If you are lucky enough to have a garden, nothing can compare with the satisfaction of nurturing a plant, enjoying it in bloom, and using the flowers to decorate and perfume your home for the rest of the year.

The technique of drying and preserving flowers and leaves dates back to the Ancient Egyptians, Greeks and Romans, who used lavishly scented mixtures of herbs, spices and flowers to

ABOVE: *Stylized flowers and foliage of every kind abound in the art of all cultures, as in this richly decorated Mogul miniature.*

LEFT: *For the ancient Egyptians, flowers were suitable offerings for the gods.*

ABOVE: *Even the most demure Victorian ladies were not so innocent as to ignore the romantic connotations of decorating with flowers.*

decorate and perfume their homes. This tradition continues today in the form of pot pourri, as popular in modern homes as it was in Victorian parlours. When suitors called, the supposedly demure young Victorian ladies would remove the lids of the large ceramic containers placed around the room to release the heady, intoxicating scents into the air.

Other flowercrafts involve capturing the fragrance of fresh flowers in oils, lotions, washballs and soaps. For centuries, flowers and herbs have been used in the street as well as the home to ward off disease and unpleasant smells. Householders used to strew sweet-smelling herbs over the rushes on their floors, and even in a modern home with fitted carpets you can add a few drops of essential oil from your favourite flower to the bag of the vacuum cleaner.

Flowers and leaves are closely associated with religious festivals and traditional celebrations, often for their symbolic significance. It is hard to imagine a wedding without floral decorations, or Christmas without holly and mistletoe, but all too often the original spirit of these decorations is lost. Make your own rose petal confetti for a wedding and rediscover the simple pleasure it will bring.

Most modern gardens are smaller than their Tudor or Victorian counterparts, and few people have a gardener to provide vast quantities of flowers for year-round displays. Many of the projects in this book are devised to create maximum impact with minimal outlay. At certain times of the year you can make the most of a seasonal glut of flowers, such as lavender, but other projects show how even a single beautiful flowerhead can be displayed to great effect. Above all, these flowercrafts are designed to be simple and enjoyable to make, leaving you with time to appreciate and savour their scents and colours.

MYTHS, MAGIC AND MYSTERY

Flowers and plants have had a long relationship with the spiritual as well as the physical side of people's lives. Many flowers were reputed to possess strange mythical properties in addition to their now-proven medicinal ones, and plant lore was widely believed in. Flowers and plants were thought to have the capacity to expel evil influences and diseases from the body. Some plants are indeed powerfully emetic or diuretic, for example, the dandelion, known as *pisse-en-lit* in France. Others, such as lavender, are potent anti-bacterials which help prevent the spread of infection in some hospitals even today.

Some plant myths seem more esoteric, but perhaps we simply do not understand, or have long since forgotten, their basis. It was once believed that fern seed made people invisible, cowslips could open locks and mandrake roots screamed when dug up. Ever since people first sought explanation for their origins and those of the world around them, they have seen symbolism and magic in the imagery of plants and trees. The Egyptians dedicated favoured flowers to the goddess Isis, while the Roman deity Flora was the custodian of blossoming plants.

The world itself has been seen as a mystic fruit of the Universe Tree or World Tree, which acted as a prop to the roof formed by the sky. Tree worship is as old as time. The Tree of Knowledge and the Tree of Life have been

ABOVE: *The Tree of Life is a universal symbol in art and legend, as in this Roman floor mosaic.*
BELOW: *The lotus flower was said to have sprung from the navel of the Hindu god Vishnu.*

venerated for centuries all over the world, the type of tree changing according to what grew in each particular climate, for example, date, cedar, fig and ash.

A lotus flower, sacred in many ancient cultures, springs symbolically from the navel of the Indian god Vishnu, and in classical mythology flowers were said to rise from the blood of dead heroes and from the teardrops of sad lovers. When Hyacinthus was struck dead by a quoit directed by Zephyr, from his blood grew the flower of the same name. The sun god Apollo inspired such an intense, unrequited love in the water nymph, Clytie, that she pined away, staring at the sun, until her limbs became rooted in the earth and her face became a sunflower, a symbol of constancy.

The seasons have also been a constant allegorical theme. Persephone, daughter of Demeter, the Earth goddess, was picking flowers when Hades carried her off to be his queen and consort in the Underworld. While her grief-stricken mother searched in vain for her daughter, plants wilted and the land grew barren. Demeter sat, inconsolable, on a stone for nine days and nights. The gods caused poppies to spring up around her feet and she breathed their scent and tasted their seeds, forgetting her sorrow in oblivious sleep. The gods intervened further and Persephone was restored to her mother for half the year, and compelled to return to Hades for the

remaining six months. Persephone is known as the seed corn, concealed within the earth, which reappears each spring and disappears again with winter. When bread is decorated with poppy seed, it symbolizes the story of Persephone and Demeter, and the cycle of the seasons and of life itself.

One of the most famous flower legends is that of Narcissus, who worshipped his own image, reflected in a pool. Attempting to reach his reflection, he drowned. The nymph Echo, who had loved him in vain, came weeping with her sister nymphs to remove his body, but it had disappeared. Only a white flower remained, floating on the surface of the water.

Indian legend tells how a Mogul emperor and his bride were walking in the palace gardens, where the long pools of water had been filled with roses to celebrate their wedding. They noticed that the heat of the sun

ABOVE: *The story of the beautiful youth Narcissus, who drowned while admiring his own reflection and became a nodding white flower at the water's edge, is one of the most beguiling flower legends.*

had produced a film of sweet-scented oil on the surface of the water. So enticing was it that they ordered it to be bottled, and so attar of roses became the perfume of emperors.

Roses have long been associated with Christ. The beautiful hellebore, or Christmas rose, has many associations and although toxic, it was once used to cure insanity. In legend, it first grew in the gardens of Heaven and was tended by the angels, who called it the "rose of love". When Paradise lay shrouded in snow, and not one flower remained in Eden, the angels asked God to let them carry it to earth as a token of His love and mercy. Another version is

that the shepherd girl Madelon came to Bethlehem and wept that the harsh winter landscape yielded no flower for her to offer the Christ Child. Gabriel touched the frozen earth with his staff and there sprang up the Christmas rose. The briar rose is reputed to have been the plant which formed the Crucifixion Crown of Thorns, and in the early days of Christian flower symbolism roses represented the blood of the martyrs. In Botticelli's painting, "The Adoration", for example, angels sprinkle rose petals over the Holy Child in a garden surrounded by roses. The Spanish gave the name Vara de Jesé to the sweetly scented tuberose, which has appeared in stained glass windows, metalwork and woodwork for centuries.

Many other tall plants, such as mullein and hollyhock, have been associated with biblical characters. The passion flower, for instance, was named to reflect Christ's Passion: the dark circle of threads which form the spectacular centre were likened to the Crown of Thorns, and the column of the ovary to the Pillar of the Cross.

The white lily has been a symbol of purity in religious art since the 12th century and, together with the rose, is often dedicated to the Virgin Mary. The iris was the Christian emblem of royalty. The columbine, with its dove-like petals, symbolizes the seven gifts of the Holy Spirit. Since the wild columbine has

ABOVE: *Angels and beautiful maidens have long been associated with flowers in art.*
BELOW RIGHT: *In his painting of the Madonna and Child, Giotto included angels holding vases of lilies and roses, symbols of the Virgin Mary in religious art since the 12th century.*

only five petals, columbines were often painted in groups of seven, particularly in early Flemish art. Botticelli is said to have been the first artist to use the humble daisy to symbolize the innocence of the newborn baby Jesus.

From the 13th century, nativity scenes have been created in churches and homes. Great care was taken in selecting the herbs to line the crib; each plant was selected for its symbolism or fragrance, and these wild flowers were given appropriate names. Collectively they were known as "cradle grasses", or "holy lay". Garden mint was called "sage of Bethlehem", and mint is linked by tradition with the Virgin Mary.

Flowers are often dedicated to saints. The choice was usually governed by availability at the time of the saint's feast, or sometimes because they grew near the saint's shrine. St David is offered the daffodil, St George the bluebell and St Swithin the Cape marigold.

Curiously, although ivy is now often used in decorations, especially at Christmas, it does not appear in Christmas legend and lore, maybe because of its pagan associations.

Holly, of course, has long-standing Christmas associations, reputed to ward off evil and representing Christ's suffering. Mistletoe

was under the care of the Scandinavian goddess of Love, hence it was ordained that all who passed under its branches should kiss.

For more practical reasons, some plants, such as lilies and artemisia, were believed to ward off evil because of their smell. Elder is considered the mother plant, and you should ask her permission before taking a bough.

Red is a colour held in universally high esteem. In many cultures it is used for protection. The rowan tree, with its scarlet berries, offers particular protection against darkness and evil. Many flowers and plants have been used as counter-charms against witches, such as the snapdragon, with its fearsome jaws, rue, and valerian.

Flowers may be regarded as good in one place and as evil in another. For example, germander speedwell is called "angel's eyes" in some parts of England, but "devil's flower" in Scotland. Many flowers were probably dedicated to the Devil because they were particularly troublesome to farmers and gardeners – field poppies are still known by some farmers as "devil's tongue".

Many spells, charms and invocations involve flowers, particularly roses, to secure the love of a desired one. Bachelor's buttons, which are also known as "knapweed", "pennywort", "ragged robin" or "red campion", featured in a very old love charm, initially used exclusively by men, but adopted by women in the 1620s.

marriage. Roses were one of the most desirous subjects of all, signifying happiness, prosperity and love. Violets promised advancement in life, but wallflowers had a diversity of meanings, depending on the dreamer – to a lover, such a dream meant that his loved one would be unfaithful, to an invalid that recovery was nigh, and to a woman who dreamt she was picking the flowers for a bouquet that the best of her admirers had yet to propose to her.

From such deeply held beliefs sprang the language of flowers, which has continued to grip the imagination of romantics to this day.

As one might expect, witches took full advantage of the broad range of properties, both physical and mystical, of flowers and plants. It was believed that no sunshine should touch a witch's herb garden, or the magical potency of the plants would be lost. Foxgloves ("witches' bells"), ragwort (which could be turned into horses), mullein and harebells all featured in the repertoire of the sorceress. The ancient art of botomancy, as this skill was known, was widely practised. White witches performed rites and ceremonies designed for more positive uses, such as soothing sick babies and protecting houses from lightning.

Many spells involving flowers were designed to induce "clear" dreams, since the prophetic properties of dreams were taken very seriously. There was even a language of dream

ABOVE: Botticelli was well aware of the symbolic meanings of flowers, and included dozens of species in his great dream of springtime and love, Primavera.
BELOW RIGHT: The rose's soft petals, sweet scent, and sharp thorns are a universal symbol of the bittersweet nature of love.

flowers, based on collective experience. To dream of box, for example, indicated long life, prosperity and a happy marriage. Dreaming of daisies in spring or summer was lucky, but the same dream in autumn was considered inauspicious. Lilies in bloom foretold marriage, but withered lilies indicated frustrated hopes and the death or severe illness of a loved one. More cheeringly, dreaming of marigolds indicated prosperity, success and a happy

THE LANGUAGE OF FLOWERS

ABOVE: *In nearly every culture, flowers are presented as offerings to the gods.*

ABOVE: *This Pre-Raphaelite painting is an example of how the language of flowers of Classical antiquity has influenced and inspired artists over the centuries.*

Although often seen as peculiarly Victorian, the language of flowers originated in the symbolism of Ancient Greek and Roman legend. As early as AD 170, the Greeks recorded their use of this form of expression and we know that they composed their garlands according to the meaning of the component plants. The Assyrians, Indians, Egyptians and Chinese all used floral symbols as a mode of communication.

In England, in the 16th century, there were many examples of verse detailing the language of flowers. "Gillyflowers for gentleness, marigolds for marriage", wrote William Hunnis. Ophelia's famous line in *Hamlet*, "There's rosemary, that's for remembrance", shows that Shakespeare knew of rosemary's medicinal use as a cure for memory loss.

Religious flower symbolism was always a dominant force in this increasingly complex

ABOVE: *The Victorians made imaginative use of the language of flowers in their greeting cards.*

and Sentiment (1857), by Arthur Freeling, attempted to uncover the origins of this fascinating language. In 1874, a more practical approach was published by Captain Marryat, author of many sea stories. *The Floral Telegraph,* or *Affection's Signals* was a highly sophisticated directory, describing how to convey incredibly specific messages with flowers. A whole sentence could be constructed by tying flowers onto a knotted cord of ribbon, in which the knots as well as the flowers had significance. Flower language booklets appeared in every bookshop and the language developed into a full-blown craze, inspiring sheet music, birthday cards, Valentine cards and some spectacularly sentimental picture postcards.

Facsimile editions of these books are still being published, and so the language of flowers lives on in each exhaustive compendium. Books on the language of flowers are by their very nature subjective. For example, as many as 30 different meanings are attributed to roses, depending on their species and colour. The following list is compiled from various sources on the language of flowers, giving the most popular or pleasing definitions.

vocabulary. A charming carol from the early 17th century explains the flower's symbolic meanings: "The Lily, white in blossom there, is Chastity; The Violet, with sweet perfume, Humility . . .".

Flower symbolism is found in folklore around the world. Aimé Martin's *Langage des Fleurs* (1830) evolved from a Turkish language of love which used other objects, such as pearls, in conjunction with flowers to convey messages. Thomas Miller published *The Poetical Language of Flowers*, or *The Pilgrimage of Love* in 1847. *Flowers, Their Use and Beauty, Language*

Anemone	*Anticipation*
Auricula	*Pride*
Bay wreath	*Reward of merit*
Bluebell	*Constancy*
Box	*Stoicism*
Broom	*Ardour*
Buttercup	*Riches*
Camellia	*Unpretending excellence*
Campanula	*Gratitude*
Carnation	*Pure Love*
Celandine	*Joy*
Chamomile	*Energy in adversity*
Chrysanthemum	*Cheerfulness*
Cinquefoil	*Maternal affection*
Clematis	*Mental beauty*
Columbine	*Resolution*
Corn	*Riches*
Crocus	*Youthful gladness*
Daffodil	*Regard*

ABOVE: *A bunch of daffodils betokens regard in the language of flowers.*

ABOVE: *The poppy, with its powerful sedative properties, represents sleep and dreams.*

ABOVE: *Daisies have symbolized innocence since ancient times.*

Jasmine	*Amiability*
Lady's mantle	*Protection*
Larkspur	*Lightness*
Lavender	*Acknowledgement of love*
Lilac	*The first stirrings of love*
Lily-of-the-valley	*Return of happiness*
Lotus	*Eloquence*
Love-lies-bleeding	*Desertion*
Lupin	*Dejection*

Daisy	*Innocence*
Dandelion	*Oracle*
Eglantine	*Simplicity*
Elder	*Zealousness*
Evening primrose	*Uncertainty*
Fern	*Sincerity*
Fern (flowering)	*Fascination*
Forget-me-not	*True love*
Gardenia	*Peace*
Geranium	*Comfort*
Harebell	*Grief*
Hawthorn	*Hope*
Hollyhock	*Ambition*
Honeysuckle	*Fidelity*
Hyacinth	*Sorrow*
Ivy	*Friendship, fidelity and marriage*

ABOVE: *Ironically, the cheering and richly scented hyacinth symbolizes sorrow.*

Magnolia	*Love of nature*
Mignonette	*Your qualities surpass your charms*
Mimosa	*Sensitivity*
Myrtle	*Love*
Nightshade	*Truth*
Orange flower	*Chastity, your purity equals your loveliness*
Pansy	*Tender and pleasant thoughts*
Pine (spruce)	*Hope in adversity*
Pink	*Perfection*
Poppy	*Sleep, dreams and fantasy*
Primrose	*Early youth*
Ranunculus	*You are rich in attractions*
Rose (damask)	*Freshness*
Rose (musk)	*Capricious beauty*
Rose (red bud)	*You are young and beautiful*
Rose (white)	*I am worthy of you*

Rosemary	*Remembrance*
Rue	*Repentance*
Sage	*Domestic virtue*
Salvia (blue)	*I think of you*
Saxifrage (mossy)	*Affection*
Scilla (blue)	*Forgive and forget*
Snowdrop	*Hope*
Star-of-Bethlehem	*Purity*
Stock	*Lasting beauty*
Sweet basil	*Good wishes*
Sweet pea	*Delicate pleasures*
Thyme	*Activity*
Tulip	*A declaration of love*
Valerian	*Accommodating disposition*
Violet	*Faithfulness*
Wallflower	*Fidelity in misfortune*
Water lily	*Purity of heart*
Wheat	*Prosperity*
Wisteria	*I cling to thee*
Xeranthemum	*Cheerfulness despite adversity*
Zinnia	*Thoughts of absent friends*

CLOCKWISE: *In view of their strong association with romantic love, it is hardly surprising that roses acquired an almost complete language of their own, with different meanings depending on their colour, shape and the way in which they were presented.*

FLOWERS FOR HEALTH AND BEAUTY

Since the earliest days of civilization, people have used flowers for their healing and curative powers. As well as their now scientifically proven efficacy and widespread acceptance as a useful complement to more conventional medicine, the flowers themselves provide great pleasure. There is something intrinsically soothing about treating oneself with such gentle, pretty remedies. (For all floral remedies, consult specialists on the subject before prescribing for yourself or others, as flowers can harm as well as cure.)

Always select prime blooms, picked at their peak of health and fragrance. Use only plants that have not been sprayed or treated with any kind of chemicals. If you are collecting hedgerow material, choose blooms that grow high up, as far away from traffic fumes as possible.

It is possible to produce essential oils and Bach-style flower remedies at home, but the demands of contemporary life often mean that you will decide to purchase at least some of your floral medicine cabinet ready-made. Any flower oils purchased for therapeutic purposes must be pure. Synthetic oils are inexpensive and may smell pleasant enough to the untrained nose, but they have no healing value

whatsoever. Homeopathic treatments can now be found in chemists, alongside non-addictive herbal sleeping pills and aromatherapy products. Authentic essential oils and subsidiary products are now even available in major supermarkets, allowing them to be introduced to an ever-widening audience.

THE FLORAL MEDICINE CABINET

The following remedies are the most popular and widely used in everyday life, and you will soon wonder how you managed without them. It is a good idea to have a separate set for travelling or at work, as well as one at home. The floral medicine cabinet is particularly useful to parents of small children, who seem to spend a disproportionately large amount of their young lives acquiring cuts, grazes and bruises. Keep all floral remedies in a cool, dark place, locked away from inquisitive hands.

PURE LAVENDER ESSENTIAL OIL

No home should be without a bottle of lavender essential oil. One of the few essential oils gentle enough to use undiluted on the skin, it has an amazing range of proven properties. Among other things, lavender is an antiseptic, antibiotic, anti-depressant and an excellent treatment for insomnia. It also has the ability to speed the regeneration of skin tissue,

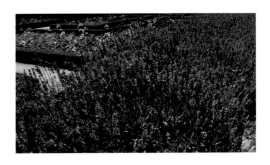

ABOVE: *Essential oil of lavender is indispensable for healing a variety of ills.*

and is a quite miraculous treatment for burns. To treat burns, run the injured area under cold water for at least 10 minutes, then drop lavender oil directly onto it. Repeat as necessary. To treat insomnia, simply apply 2 drops of lavender oil to a pillowcase (no more, as it would begin to have a stimulant effect), or 1 drop to the back of a fractious child's pyjamas. A couple of drops added to an already run, warm (not hot) bath is a gloriously sybaritic way of curing insomnia.

PURE PEPPERMINT ESSENTIAL OIL

This essential oil is universally recognized as a wonderful cure for indigestion and heartburn. Take 1 drop in warm water, sweetened with honey, for fast relief; alternatively, add 2 drops to a bowl of boiling water and inhale the vapour. It has also been proved that the aroma of peppermint oil improves concentration – use it at work or inhale it directly from the bottle when you are driving for long periods.

PURE TEA TREE ESSENTIAL OIL

Tea tree ranks alongside lavender for its wide range of practical, everyday applications. It is anti-bacterial, anti-viral and a powerful stimulant to the immune system. It is a very effective treatment for fungal conditions such as thrush and athlete's foot, as well as treating everything from toothache to cold sores. Tea tree oil can irritate sensitive skin, so apply it with caution initially. At the first sign of a cold or influenza, add 3 drops to a warm, already run bath (1 drop for a child), and you may find this sufficient to ward off the illness altogether.

PURE ELEMI ESSENTIAL OIL

Although eucalyptus oil is a better-known decongestant for the misery of a blocked-up nose, its stimulant qualities can be unwelcome if you are trying to get to sleep. Elemi shares the same powerfully decongestant properties without keeping you awake all night.

ECHINACEA TINCTURE

This simple herbal tincture, produced from the purple coneflower, can prevent a sniffle turning into a full-blown cold if taken in time.

ABOVE: *The fresh juice of the common pot marigold may be squeezed directly on to broken skin to ease pain and assist healing.*

CALENDULA CREAM AND TINCTURE

The humble marigold (*Calendula officinalis*) is a great healer. It is used both homeopathically and in herbalism. As a tincture or infusion, it is very gentle and is perfect for applications where the skin is broken and painful to touch. Apply the tincture first, moving on to the soothing cream when the patient can stand the area being touched. Add a drop of lavender to prevent scarring and to aid regeneration of the skin tissue. Gentle massage also promotes healing by stimulating the circulation.

ARNICA TABLETS AND OINTMENT

Arnica is a wonderful remedy for shock and bruises. It is indispensable in homes where there are children – or an inexpert DIY fanatic.

BACH RESCUE REMEDY

Dr Edward Bach's simple, safe, yet profoundly effective floral remedies are now available in high street chemists as well as health food shops and by mail order. An essential for the first aid cabinet and handbag is the Rescue Remedy, a combination of five of his 38 remedies – cherry, plum, impatiens, rock rose and star-of-Bethlehem. This safe, all-purpose emergency treatment is useful for all kinds of shock, and also for stressful events such as visiting the dentist or taking a driving test. A few drops may be taken directly from the bottle or mixed in a glass of water. Like Arnica, Rescue Remedy is perfect for carrying with you if you have small children.

CHAMOMILLA

This homeopathic derivative of the chamomile plant is especially useful for teething babies. It is available in individual sachets which children accept readily. It calms even the most irritable or anxious child, and is perfect for use in combination with chamomile essential oil, which may be applied in compresses, as an inhalation or in a bath.

The
STILL
ROOM

LADIES FAIR, I BRING TO YOU
LAVENDER WITH SPIKES OF BLUE;
SWEETER PLANT WAS NEVER FOUND
GROWING ON AN ENGLISH GROUND.

Caryl Battersby in A Bunch of Sweet Lavender,
Constance Isherwood, 1900

ABOVE AND LEFT: *Candlewax, soap and a
few other simple ingredients can be utterly
transformed by combining them with flowers and
flower essences, with their delicate fragrances and
healing powers.*

21

INTRODUCTION

The Elizabethans knew that certain flowers and herbs, and their essential oils, had the power to ward off infection and discourage pests and vermin, as well as smelling beautiful. In those days, poor sanitation, sporadic personal hygiene and widespread disease meant that the lady of the house would derive great pleasure from creating products to perfume her home and keep it as free from pests and germs as possible.

Throughout history, the well-stocked still room has flourished, supplying a wealth of scented remedies based on flowers and herbs from the garden. Lavender, orange-flower and rose waters were used to rinse linen, and were taken internally as medicine. In stronger concentrations, they were placed in casting bottles, to perfume clean linen before storing it. Roses and lavender have always been important ingredients in the still room; not only do they smell delightful, but lavender is a fly and moth repellent. Lavender stalks were woven with ribbon and given in betrothal sets of 12; these were then used to mark dozens and half-dozens of linen in the dowry chest.

"Sweet pots" or pot pourri (literally "rotten pot" in French) have been used since medieval times to perfume the often noxious air of

ABOVE: *Harvest your own garden flowers at their summer best.*

castles and manor houses. Moist pot pourri, although initially taking longer to prepare than the dry version, lasts amazingly well and is worth the additional effort. As well as supplying finished preparations, the still room was also where flowers and herbs were prepared and stored for use during the long winter months.

Today, flowers are flown from one corner of the world to another to ensure that our homes need never be without colour, but their fragrance is often non-existent. How much more satisfying to fill your home with sweet-scented offerings from your own garden – in the depths of winter, every time you open your airing cupboard the scent of peppermint and lavender will lift your spirits, recalling the long summer days when you gathered the flowers and prepared them for

drying. The modern version of an Elizabethan still room may be little more than a crowded kitchen work surface and a clothes airer suspended from the ceiling, but it will provide year-round colour and scent throughout your home, and be the source of countless gifts for family and friends.

ABOVE AND LEFT: *Flowers and pure flower oils are a delightfully traditional way to perfume cosmetics and toiletries. Use them to scent luxurious gifts such as Tudor Wash Balls.*

Choosing and Preparing Flowers

The chief thing to remember when choosing flowers for any type of flowercraft, from a single bloom in a jamjar for the kitchen table to a more labour-intensive arrangement on a grand scale for a big celebration, is to enjoy the whole experience, from concept to completion. Wise was the man or woman who said that we should "take time to smell the roses". There is no point at all in producing some fabulously stunning floral arrangement if you are so exhausted at the end of your endeavours that you cannot enjoy the special occasion you are celebrating.

Choose flowers for their fragrance, their colour, their shape but, above all, let your decision be an emotional one. Choose flowers because you love them, because the soaring blue of delphiniums gladdens your heart, or the smell of an old-fashioned damask rose sets your head reeling. Do not discard flowers simply because they are not perfect – a single, rain-damaged rose, sprinkled with gold and taupe freckles, is in itself a thing of great beauty. Placed in a Russian tea glass with a gilded rim and translucent painted decoration, it becomes a work of art.

In addition to aesthetic matters, there are some more down-to-earth considerations to bear in mind, which will help to prolong the life of fresh flowers and to produce optimum results when you are preserving flowers for later use.

ABOVE: *Much loved, well-worn tools enhance the joys of growing and harvesting in your own garden.*

HARVESTING

If you are picking flowers for drying, there are very specific guidelines as to when to pick each species for the best results. A flower may shrivel if picked a few days too early, or fade and droop if left fractionally too long. It is well worth investing in a specialist book on this subject if you plan to become more seriously involved.

As a rule, choose flowers at the peak of their perfection, but just before the petals fall – the French call this *à point*. Gather flowers in the morning, when the sun has caused the dew to evaporate and encouraged the fragrance to develop, but before there is a danger of wilting. Ideally, have a container of water with you to hold your harvest. Staunch the flow of sap from glutinous-stemmed plants such as daffodils and euphorbia by dipping the stems in soil before placing them in the water.

If you are preserving the flowers, start immediately, ignoring the conditioning that is so vital to the long life of fresh cut flowers.

CONDITIONING CUT FLOWERS

Just as apprentice hairdressers have to shampoo countless heads of hair before being allowed near a pair of scissors, florists spend a large part of their initial training learning how to condition flowers, long before they progress to arranging them. Without proper conditioning, the most healthy of cut flowers will die without achieving their full potential.

The rules are the same, whether you are dealing with garden flowers or blooms from a florist. Re-cut the stems, remove all foliage which will be below the waterline, then plunge the stems into a bucket of deep water to allow

them to have a good, long drink. Wrap the heads and upper stems of some flowers in paper while they are having their drink - this helps tulips to stay straight, and delicate flowers benefit from this gentle support around their fragile necks. The sap of some flowers, such as euphorbia, continues to flow after the stem has been cut and is an irritant, as well as producing unsightly cloudy water. Singe the stem end over a naked flame for 10 seconds, which forces any moisture in the stem upwards to the flower and breaks down any airlock that might be present. The burnt end is now charcoal, through which water can still pass. Treat poppies in the same way. Stand the bucket in a cool, draught-free room, in the dark if you wish to retard the development of the blooms, or in indirect light to accelerate blossoming. During the conditioning time, which should be a minimum of 6 hours, check that the flowers are taking up water. Drooping foliage and limp heads indicate an airlock – roses are particularly susceptible to this problem.

FIRST AID FOR WILTING FLOWERS

Heat a small pan of water to boiling point. Wrap your hand and the flowerhead in a cloth to protect both from the steam, then plunge the ends of the stems into the water for 10 seconds. Return the flowers to the conditioning bucket.

ABOVE: A bunch of lavender on the kitchen door deters flies as well as smelling sweet.
RIGHT: Children love gardening and decorating with flowers if given their own small tools and the freedom to experiment.

STEM TREATMENT

All stems must be cut again before the flowers are placed in the display container. Research has shown that a single, diagonal cut provides the best uptake of water. Fill the hollow stems of flowers such as delphiniums with water and plug the ends with cottonwool.

Remove the stamens from lilies, as they stain everything they come into contact with, including the petals of the flower itself. Cut off closed buds at the top of a stem, as they will steal water from the rest of the flower but are unlikely to open before the main bloom dies.

FLOWER FOOD

The packets of food that are sold alongside cut flowers are not just a gimmick. They are a precisely balanced blend of food and anti-bacterial agents which nurture the flowers, as well as keeping the water in the vase or container clean and germ-free. Similar results can be achieved with a drop of bleach and a small amount of sugar, but it seems wisest to opt for the pre-measured commercial dose. Directions for use are given on the packet.

DRYING FLOWERS

*T*he object in drying flowers is always to achieve dried fresh flowers, not dry dead flowers. The key is to remember that you need to remove the moisture from the flower or other plant material as quickly as possible.

AIR-DRYING

This is the simplest form of flower preservation, requiring no specialist materials or expertise and excellent for beginners. Moisture is removed from the petals by the circulation of air, using no preservative.

RIGHT: *Large flowers like roses dry best hung head down in small bunches.*

BELOW: *To retain the natural arching habit of a plant, dry the stems upright.*

If you are intending to make pot pourri, separate the petals from the flowers as soon as you have gathered them and spread them out on trays for air-drying.

Fasten each small bunch of flowers with an elastic band – this will contract as the stems dry and shrink and continue to hold them securely.

Remove large leaves as they will look shrivelled and unattractive when dried; smaller leaves can be removed by rubbing them off after drying.

The golden rule is that the flowers must be dry, with no residual moisture from rain or dew. Choose perfect specimens only, as imperfections look unsightly in preserved work. Remove any large leaves, as they become shrivelled and unattractive when dried; smaller leaves can be removed by rubbing them off after drying.

HANGING METHOD
Gather the stems into small bunches – not too large or they will rot. Fasten each bunch with elastic bands, which will contract as the stems dry and shrink. Hang the bunches head down in a dry, dark, airy place.

STANDING METHOD
Some forms of plant material are best dried upright, so that their pendulous nature is preserved. Simply prepare them as normal and place in a container.

"ARRANGE AND DRY"
Hydrangeas, molucella and erica respond well to this alternative method of air-drying. It is only suitable for fully mature stems, otherwise the flowers will shrivel and curl unattractively. Place them in a container with 2.5 cm (1 in) or so of water, and allow them to take up the water and then dry out.

ABOVE: *Sturdy sunflowers dry beautifully for dramatic arrangements with an echo of hot summer sunshine.*

PRESERVING FLOWERS AND LEAVES

WIRING FLOWERS BEFORE PRESERVING

Dried flowers are so delicate that it is a good idea to wire them when fresh if you wish to use them later in an arrangement. Many flowers have succulent stems which collapse when the moisture is removed, and need the support of florist's wires if they are to be arranged successfully. Others, such as roses, appear to have firm stems but these can become weak just below the head after preserving, causing the flowers to flop. It is wise, therefore, to push a short length of stub wire up each stem before desiccant-preserving.

As the flower dries, the plant material shrinks onto the wire, which corrodes slightly on contact with the sap, making the bond very secure. The preserved flower can then be easily lengthened by adding more wire before arranging. Flat leaves, such as rose leaves, can also be wired into more interesting shapes by binding their bases around a stub wire while they are fresh and flexible.

PRESERVING FOLIAGE IN GLYCERINE

As with air-drying, choose perfect specimens that are free from rain or dew. If you like, you can place the container in a bucket so that it will not topple over when you add the foliage.

Stand the container in a warm, dry, dark place. Check it every day and top up with fresh glycerine mixture if necessary. You will notice the foliage changing colour as the glycerine is gradually absorbed. The aim is to remove it at exactly the point when it has fully absorbed the mixture, but no later. Over-glycerining will make the leaves look oily and encourage mildew. Wipe the stems dry the moment they are removed from the mixture. If you do over-glycerine, remove the foliage and immerse it in warm water with a drop of washing-up liquid,

USING GLYCERINE

1   Choose a container large enough to take the foliage and add the glycerine.

2   Top this up with 2 parts hot water to 1 part glycerine, to a depth of 8 cm (3 in). Mix well.

3   For wood-stemmed foliage, cut and split the stem ends then place in the glycerine mixture immediately. For calyces, seedheads, herbaceous foliage and soft-stemmed leaves, allow the mixture to cool first.

rinse, shake off the excess water and stand in a warm place to dry. The glycerine mixture can be sieved, re-heated and re-used.

To store glycerine-preserved foliage, do not use polythene boxes or plastic bags, as mildew may form inside. Ask a florist for the boxes in which fresh flowers are delivered, with holes in the sides for air circulation. Hang up seedheads and calyces which might be squashed if laid flat, or stand them upright in jamjars.

DESICCANT PRESERVING

Desiccants are peerless at preserving the natural colour and shape of flowers, and are well worth mastering. A desiccant is a substance which removes moisture – sand, starch, cornmeal, alum and detergent powder have all been used for drying flowers. The two most popular desiccants used today are silica gel and borax.

Silica gel absorbs up to 50 per cent of its own weight in moisture, and is used industrially for this purpose. Although it is more expensive than borax, it has the distinct advantage that it does not need heat. Chemists stock silica gel, but usually in the form of crystals which are so coarse that they mark the flowers badly. It is difficult to grind the crystals down and they give off a hazardous dust, so it is far better to use the silica gel that is specifically marketed for flowers. This often has a colour marker, making it very easy to see when the crystals have absorbed their own

ABOVE: *Preserving foliage in glycerine produces a wealth of interesting plant material for arrangements.*

weight in moisture. They then need to be reactivated by warming them in an oven, following the manufacturer's instructions. The silica gel can then be re-used over and over. Borax is inexpensive and readily available, but it has the disadvantage of requiring a constant temperature of 75°F (24°C). Being a powder, it also tends to cling. It does not draw out moisture as efficiently as silica gel, so the flowers take much longer to dry and often become discoloured in the process. Borax is best used if you have a large quantity of

thin-petalled flowers, which will dry quickly.

Choose flowers that are not quite open, as those that are fully open will fall when the flower is dried. As with air-drying, pick them after the sun has dried the dew from the petals but before the midday sun has made the flowers wilt. Preserve the flowers as soon as possible after harvesting. As you harvest, place them in moist florist's foam or in a container of water, keeping the heads dry.

USING DESICCANT

Spoon a layer of either silica gel or borax desiccant into a container to a depth of 1 cm (½ in); for silica gel, use an airtight container. Always preserve only one layer of flowers in each container to avoid damaging them. It is also a good idea to dry only one species of flower in each container, so that you can gauge the drying time by examining one flower without disturbing the rest – desiccant-preserved flowers are very fragile. Leaves are simpler in form and more robust and can be dried in layers, with 1 cm (½ in) of desiccant between each layer.

Place flowers with simple, flat faces, such as daisies, face down. Roses and other more rounded flowers are best dried face up, as are flowers that are only partially open. Bell- or trumpet-shaped flowers, such as hollyhocks, need to be dried on their sides. Flower spikes, such as delphiniums, which have florets around the whole stem, need protection so that the florets do not become crushed. Place them across supporting ridges of folded cardboard, with the stems resting in notches. Bell- or trumpet-shaped flowers need to be carefully filled with desiccant before placing them on their sides, so that they do not become crushed.

Borax is lighter than silica gel and can be safely spooned directly on top of the flowers, but it is sensible to use the same method in case you forget which desiccant you are using!

The length of drying time depends on the density of each flower. As a rough guide, miniature flowers may be dry in 3-4 days, roses in 7-10 days, while fleshy flowers such as orchids may take 2-3 weeks. To test the flowers for readiness, gently scrape back the desiccant and remove a single flower. If all looks well, hold it to your ear and flick it gently – if it makes a crisp, papery sound, it is dry. Carefully pour off the desiccant through your fingers and catch each flower by its stem. Stand it in a container or push the stem into a block of florist's foam. Gently remove any residual desiccant with a small, soft paintbrush. You can leave a small amount of desiccant in the centre of large flowerheads, to absorb any remaining moisture. Re-attach fallen petals with a tiny dab of contact adhesive.

Leaving flowers even longer in either desiccant will not produce correspondingly better results. When the moisture has been removed from the petals, they become very fragile and will simply disintegrate.

STORING DESICCANT PRESERVED FLOWERS

Damp environments, such as steamy bathrooms and kitchens, will cause desiccant-preserved flowers to flop, but most normal household conditions are suitable. You can apply a commercially available spray to protect flowers from damp and dust. Apply sparingly, when the flowers have just been removed from the desiccant and are perfectly clean and dry, otherwise you will seal in moisture and dirt.

If you are not arranging the flowers immediately, store them with their stems wedged into florist's foam on a high shelf in a heated airing cupboard. Alternatively, lay them in rows in a sealed airtight tin, each stem poked through a hole in a strip of cardboard placed

USING SILICA GEL

1 Spoon the desiccant carefully around the flower. Do not pour it over the top as the sudden weight would crush the form of the flower.

2 As you continue sprinkling, the crystals will gradually cover the flower. Go on until there is a 1 cm (½ in) layer on top of the plant.

3 Cover with kitchen foil, sealing it with tape to make it airtight. Label with the plant name and the date, to avoid confusion later.

USING BORAX

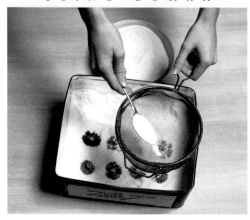

1 Sprinkle borax around the flowers through a sieve to remove any lumps, so that it flows as freely as table salt.

2 Do not cover the container. Label it and place in a constant temperature of 75°F (24°C), for example in a heated airing cupboard.

across the tin, so that the head does not become crushed. Sprinkle a small amount of desiccant over the base of the tin to absorb any residual moisture from the flower centres.

PRESSING FLOWERS

The same rules apply to harvesting flowers for pressing as for dried flowers. Choose flowers in peak condition, with no hint of moisture. Take jamjars and water with you, and place the stems in just enough water to keep them fresh but not so much that the petals become damp.

Collect flowers at various stages of their life cycle so that you have an interesting range of colours and blossoms. There are no set rules about what to press, or when during the year to harvest. From the first tentative buds of spring to the splendour of autumn leaves, there are year-round opportunities for pressing, although late summer yields the greatest variety. Experimenting is half the fun, so try everything! Remember to respect the countryside – pick only a small amount of flowers, and do not harm the plant itself.

Press leaves, stems and flowerheads together unless they vary greatly in thickness. In such instances, press the thicker parts on separate sheets of blotting paper. Very bulky heads, such as rosebuds and sea holly heads, are best sliced in half before pressing and used separately. Some flowers, for example pansies, can be divided into individual petals before pressing,

then re-assembled into approximations of the original flower.

Check that each piece has sufficient room to spread evenly under the weight of the press as it dries, and that it is not being crushed by other plant material. Remove damaged leaves, and do not allow the plant material to protrude beyond the blotting paper. Ideally, leave at least a 2.5 cm (1 in) gap around the edges so that all the pieces are pressed consistently.

Whether you use a flower press or press your flowers between the pages of heavy books, you will need a large quantity of blotting paper. Commercial flower presses hold only a small amount of flowers, so they are ideal for field trips but less useful for pressing larger quantities. You can make a press from wood and strong, unridged cardboard. Label and date each flower on pieces of paper protruding from the press.

Pansies may be divided into separate petals for pressing and reassembled for display.

31

WIRING AND TAPING

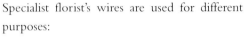

This aspect of working with flowers often seems full of mysterious technicalities known only to professional florists. Wiring is, in fact, quite simple and the results are very versatile – you can make stems any length you wish and curve them at any angle, so that even complex projects such as wreaths and garlands become easy to achieve. Wires are essential when flowers need to be positioned at precise angles, for example, in wedding bouquets and headdresses. They can also support flowers with heavy heads, or be used to attach non-flowering materials, such as fruit, fir cones and nuts, to a display.

Specialist florist's wires are used for different purposes:

STUB WIRES serve to reinforce stems.

FINE REEL or SILVER WIRE is used to bind lightweight plant materials, and is especially useful in bridal displays where delicacy and lightness are important.

MEDIUM-GAUGE REEL WIRE is a good all-purpose binding wire. Use it to assemble small bunches of flowers ready to attach to a larger arrangement, or to bind moss onto a wreath base.

THICK REEL WIRE is used for larger pieces, for example, securing heads of maize and other vegetables.

Fresh flowers can be wired internally or externally. Dried flowers are, as a rule, too delicate for internal wiring.

INTERNAL WIRING

This is the most suitable method for wiring heavy flowerheads, for example, roses. Insert a fine wire into the stem, pushing it up and through the flowerhead to form a hook. Pull the wire back down, embedding the hook in the flowerhead. Bind this wired stem to a thicker wire appropriate to the arrangement you are creating.

LEFT: *Just a few inexpensive materials and some simple techniques are all you will need, even to achieve elaborate effects.*

WIRING AND TAPING

1   Strip the leaves from the flower stem. Keep the florist's tape in a sealed bag to keep the adhesive tacky.

4   Bind this wired stem with florist's tape. Hold the tape at the top of the flowerhead then pull down, stretching the tape to release the adhesive as you wind.

2   Cut off the stem at the flowerhead, leaving just a short length. Insert a wire through the remaining stem.

5   Continue binding to the end of the wire and finish off neatly. The florist's tape strengthens the wired stems, as well as disguising them.

3   Push the wire up through the stem, right into the flower. Form a hook and pull back down, embedding the hook in the flowerhead.

EXTERNAL WIRING

Some flowers, such as freesias, can be wired by winding a fine silver wire round and through the flower itself, then making a double leg mount as a reinforced stem (see below).

SINGLE AND DOUBLE LEG MOUNTS

Use single leg mounts for smaller flowers. Take a medium-gauge wire and bend the top 2.5 cm (1 in) into a "U" shape. Bind the "U" and the shortened flower stem together with the long end of the wire. For a double leg mount, double a heavy-gauge wire, place the "U" shape against the flower stem, then wind one half of the doubled leg round the other.

For
EMBELLISHING
the HOME

I BRING FRESH SHOWERS FOR

THE THIRSTING FLOWERS,

FROM THE SEAS AND THE STREAMS.

(P.B. Shelley, 1792-1822)

ABOVE AND LEFT: *Creative floral
centrepieces provide an eye-catching focal point
for any room.*

3 5

INTRODUCTION

Flowers and foliage bring the glories of Nature into the home.
They cheer even the dullest winter's day, diffusing their potent
fragrances through every room to evoke memories of high summer.

For centuries, people have decorated their homes with greenery and flowers, both to celebrate nature and to soften the hard edges of what was often a hostile environment. The love of flowers in the home reached a zenith in the 19th century; the Victorians adored garden flowers and brought them indoors in a great diversity of forms. Pressed, waxed, dried, fresh or as pot plants, flowers filled every surface of the cluttered Victorian interior. Dried flower arrangements which survive from the 19th century often have a gloomy, funereal air, partly because mourning was a presiding fashion after the death of Prince Albert. When Queen Victoria died, the flowers that had decorated her bedroom were pressed, made into cards and sent to those close to her.

In fact, preserving summer flowers is a delightful occupation, requiring neither special equipment nor expertise.

ABOVE: *Even the simplest flower*
arrangement adds a touch of colour.

A visit to a floristry supplier's warehouse for inspiration is recommended, and many specialist suppliers are happy to sell to the public. There you will find sensibly sized reels of florist's wire, florist's scissors to cut through wire as well as stems, packs of dried fruit slices, tiny terracotta pots, florist's tape in every conceivable colour, armfuls of eucalyptus and lavender . . . the list is endless. Supplement these with flowers from your own and friends' gardens – peonies, in particular, make spectacular centrepieces in dried arrangements.

Of course, fresh-cut flowers and foliage will always be the cheapest and quickest facelift a room can have. Whether you place a few daisies in a jamjar or fill a crystal vase with show-stopping blooms such as lilies or parrot tulips, flowers take centre stage in any decor. Their fleeting beauty is part of their charm. With each day, there is a subtle

change – a few petals fall as confetti onto the table below, and tightly furled buds open to reveal majestic blooms. We often cease to see our everyday surroundings, familiarity breeding, if not contempt, then a certain laziness, so it is vital to inject new life and interest. Even a single flower will focus the attention and bring a moment of stillness to the hectic pace of modern living.

Flowers have their place in every room in the house. Choose their colour and fragrance to suit your interior design schemes and the personalities of the inhabitants.

ABOVE: *The lily is ideal for formal arrangements.* LEFT: *The sunflower is a potent symbol of laid-back summer days.*

MOSSY PICTURE FLOWER FRAME

Make a special posy of flowers the centre of attention – these were picked by a child for her mother, and are said to bring luck. Cover an old picture frame with fresh green moss, studded with star-like white allium flowers. Moss is available from garden centres, but if you collect it yourself remember to take only a little from different sites so that it will regenerate.

g a t h e r

glue gun
moss
old picture frame
florist's scissors
artificial allium flowerhead

1 Working on a protected surface, glue large pieces of moss onto the picture frame, pressing the moss well into any moulded areas.

2 Snip individual florets from the artificial allium flowerhead, leaving stems of about 1 cm (¹/₂ in).

IT MIGHT WELL BE SAID OF ME THAT HERE I HAVE MERELY MADE UP A BUNCH OF OTHER MEN'S FLOWERS, AND PROVIDED NOTHING OF MY OWN BUT THE STRING TO BIND THEM.

(Michel de Montaigne, 1533-92)

3 Glue the allium florets randomly on top of the moss, pressing the stems well into the soft moss.

GERBERA CUSHION

*B*ring a splash of colour to a dark or dull corner of your living room by using three hot shades of the same flower – fuchsia, tangerine and cherry red. Dismantle artificial gerbera flowers to obtain flat flowerheads to stitch onto the cushion, then reassemble the flowers. The cushion fabric is simple linen scrim, which makes a sophisticated background to the vivid colours. Arrange the flowers in a regular pattern for maximum impact.

g a t h e r

2 pieces of linen scrim fabric,
each 60 cm (24 in) square
dressmaker's pins
sewing machine
matching sewing threads
iron
cushion pad, 50 cm (20 in) square
tape measure
dressmaker's pencil
sewing needle
9 artificial gerbera flowers: 4 fuchsia,
3 tangerine, 2 cherry red
scissors
scalpel
ultra-high-tack PVA glue

Place the two linen squares right sides together. Pin, then machine stitch round three sides. Turn right side out and press. Insert the cushion pad.

Mark a border round all four sides, then top stitch close to the pad. Slip stitch the open edge.

Dismantle each gerbera flowerhead, discarding the rigid plastic cup (the calyx). Using a scalpel, slice through the remaining, softer part of each calyx so that the flower will sit flat. Stitch the flowers to the cushion in a regular pattern, stitching through the middle, then glue the centres back in place. Undo the slip stitching to remove the pad for cleaning.

40

GILDED PLANT SAMPLER

This is an updated version of the botanical samplers which were so popular in Victorian times. The lively, spontaneous mix of natural materials includes chilli peppers, rose petals, kaffir lime leaves and spices, all of which are very fragrant. Decorate the sampler with richly coloured embroidery threads, and finish with a few restrained touches of gold leaf, or picture framer's gold paint.

Pull threads from the edges of the hessian to make a fringe all round. Glue horizontal lines of twine on top, then vertical lines, to make a grid pattern. Tie knots at a few intersections. Glue the chilli peppers, petals, leaves and spices in the grid squares, applying tiny amounts of glue with a cocktail stick. Work running stitch and cross stitch through some of the leaves and petals. Apply gilding size and metal leaf to a few areas; alternatively, use gold paint.

gather

piece of hessian, 20 x 30 cm (8 x 12 in)

ultra-high-tack PVA glue

fine jute twine, scissors

6 dried chilli peppers

12 fresh or dried yellow rose petals

6 dried kaffir lime leaves

3 blades of dried mace

3 star anise

cocktail stick

embroidery needle

embroidery threads: burgundy and gold

Dutch metal gold leaf and gilding size or picture framer's gold paint and brush

41

EUCALYPTUS LAMPSHADE

Eucalyptus has the most deliciously uplifting scent and the soft grey-green leaves tone beautifully with modern interiors. This lampshade edging is simplicity itself to do and the preserved leaves last well. The heat of the lightbulb will bring out the cool, refreshing scent, creating a sanctuary in a corner of your room for reading or sewing.

g a t h e r

branch of preserved eucalyptus leaves
florist's scissors
glue gun
plain lampshade

1   Working on a protected surface, divide the eucalyptus branch into individual stems. Remove any damaged leaves.

2   Glue the stems round the bottom edge of the lampshade, with each stem facing the same way. Hold each stem firmly in place until the glue has set.

LAVENDER–FILLED BUCKET

Many projects in this book celebrate the medicinal properties of lavender, its taste and its fragrance. Lavender is also a very beautiful plant, with silvery grey foliage and flowers in shades from pale pink to indigo. Simply stacked in bunches, it makes a wonderful display. Grow as much as you can and beg extra from your neighbours' gardens – you will need approximately 400 stalks to fill this 10 cm (4 in) diameter bucket. Finish with a metal mesh "bow", cut with tin snips. The decorative mulch round the edge is pea shingle.

gather

craft knife
florist's dry foam
galvanized bucket, 10 cm (4 in) in diameter
stems of dried lavender
florist's scissors

1   Cut a block of foam to fit across the bucket and end just below the rim.

2   Make up bunches of approximately 25 lavender stems. Turn each bunch upside down and tap it gently on the work surface to level off the flowerheads.

3   Gauge the finished height of the display by holding each bunch against the bucket. Cut the stems to the required length. Push each bunch firmly into the foam, packing them close together.

44

LEAFY BOWER LIGHT SWITCH

*M*ake a feature of a light switch with a decoration of rain-soaked leaves. Dry brush the surrounding wall, using two shades of eucalyptus-coloured paint, then apply the leaves in a random design as if they had just blown in through the window. Soak the leaves for at least a week in rainwater to soften them.

g a t h e r

fine sandpaper
brass light switch
emulsion paints: dark and pale eucalyptus
paintbrush
selection of leaves, soaked in rainwater
kitchen paper
PVA glue
fine paintbrush, for glue

1 Lightly sand the light switch and surrounding wall. Paint with dark eucalyptus and leave to dry. Using a dry brush, paint a thin coat of pale eucalyptus on top, allowing the base coat to show through.

2 Remove each leaf from the rainwater and blot the excess water on kitchen paper. Using a fine paintbrush, apply glue generously to the back of the leaf.

3 Position each leaf carefully across the light switch, pressing it well into any moulded details. Dilute 3 parts glue with 1 part water, and brush over the surface of the leaf and surrounding area.

TULLE FLOWER SCREEN

*H*ide a less-than-lovely view with this delicate miniature screen. Make up each panel separately, as many as you require, using ivory-coloured tulle stretched across a beech-wood frame. The panels are then hinged together with ivory-coloured ribbon ties. Decorate the screen with sprigs of gypsophila flowers, simply stitched in place. Tulle is available in a delicious range of colours from lemon sorbet to jelly bean pink, so you can adapt the colour scheme and the flowers to suit your decor.

g a t h e r

(FOR EACH PANEL)

2 pieces of white beech, each
20 cm x 12 mm x 12 mm (8 x ¹/₂ x ¹/₂ in)
2 pieces of white beech, each
30 cm x 12 mm x 12 mm (12 x ¹/₂ x ¹/₂ in)
drill and drill bit, slightly smaller than
the panel pins
wood glue
4 panel pins
2 pieces of ivory tulle, each
40 x 26 cm (16 x 10¹/₄ in)
staple gun
2 lengths of ivory silk ribbon, each 50 cm (20 in)
preserved yellow gypsophila
sewing needle
sewing thread, to match gypsophila stems
scissors

To make up the panel, place the two short lengths of wood outside the longer ones. Drill pilot holes through the short pieces where they will be panel-pinned to the long pieces, to prevent the wood from splitting. Drill two holes through one of the long pieces from front to back, for the ribbon ties (follow the illustrations for position). Glue and then pin the frame together. Stretch both pieces of tulle over the frame in a double layer, and staple to the back. Stitch the gypsophila onto the tulle with tiny stitches through the stems. Hinge the panels together, using the ribbon ties.

48

BLEACHED LEAVES

As well as drying and preserving leaves, you can completely remove their colour, using ordinary household bleach. The resulting ghostly white leaves make a very quick and effective window decoration, applied directly to the glass. For an enchanting Christmas decoration, surround the bleached leaves with white fairy lights and add glass drops or beads suspended on silver thread from the window frame.

gather

disposable plastic gloves
selection of fresh leaves
bowl or container
bleach
wooden skewer
piece of glass or windowpane
kitchen paper

1   Working on a protected surface and wearing plastic gloves, immerse the leaves in bleach until they have lost all their colour. Use a skewer to make sure the leaves are fully submerged.

2   Smooth the leaves onto the glass. Gently wipe away any excess bleach with kitchen paper. Leave to dry.

FLOWERHEAD JUG COVER

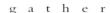

*A*lthough most homes no longer have a pantry or a larder, old-fashioned beaded milk jug covers are still very useful today for deflecting the unwanted attentions of insects. This simple muslin square, sprinkled with fresh white daisies and weighed down at the corners with glistening drops of clear glass and pearl, is an elegant modern version of an old favourite. Make the same design in a larger size to cover jugs of homemade lemonade or elderflower cordial.

g a t h e r

square of white muslin fabric, large enough
to drape comfortably over the jug
sewing needle
sewing threads: white and green
scissors
round glass beads
artificial pearl beads
artificial daisies

2   Using white thread, stitch a few beads to each corner of the muslin square. Keep the weight approximately the same at each corner.

1   Pull an equal number of threads from each side of the muslin square to make an attractive fringed border.

MEADOWS TRIM WITH DAISIES PIED,

SHALLOW BROOKS AND RIVERS WIDE.

(John Milton, 1608-74)

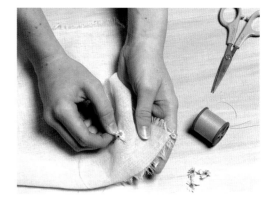

3   Snip the daisy flowerheads from the stems, leaving 1 cm (¹/₂ in) stems. Using green thread, stitch the daisies in a random design onto the muslin square, passing the needle through the stems.

50

PRESSED FLOWER CANDLES

Nothing is more magical on a still summer's evening than eating or entertaining by candlelight. A theatrical effect can be simply created by placing several candles in glass jars on a baking tray, so that its metal surface reflects the shimmering flames as they burn down. Scatter fragrant flowers such as elderflowers and roses round the display, to make the most of their short-lived beauty and heady scent, which will be enhanced by the heat of the candles – remember not to leave lit candles unattended. Any small pressed flowers would be suitable for this project.

g a t h e r

white wax candles
tea towel
metal spoon
cup of boiling water
pressed primrose flowers and leaves
transparent glue
cheese grater
double boiler
metal kitchen tongs

Place each candle on a folded tea towel for stability. Heat the metal spoon in a cup of boiling water and rub the spoon over the candle, to soften the wax. Press a leaf in place, using the back of the spoon. Continue until the layer of leaves is complete. Glue the flowers on top, using a minimal amount of transparent glue. Coarsely grate another candle and melt the wax in a double boiler. Using the tongs, hold the decorated candle by the wick and dip it in the molten wax for a few seconds. Smooth over the surface of the flowers and leaves with your fingertip while the wax is still soft. Leave to cool and then repeat, holding the other end of the candle.

DAISY CHAIN WALL BORDER

Commercial wall borders have become so ubiquitous that their appeal has been almost lost. This pretty daisy design adds interest and sparkle to a wall, without the uniformity of a straight paper border. It is worked over a base of gold tissue paper, which gives added texture, then sprayed with a shimmering veil of gold, copper and green paint. Aim for transparent rather than solid colour. Instead of daisies, you can use any pressed flowers to fit in with your overall decorating scheme.

gather

PVA glue
disposable plastic container
large and small paintbrushes
sheets of gold tissue paper
pressed daisy flowers and leaves
tweezers
spray paints: gold, copper and green

Dilute 3 parts glue with 1 part water. Using a large paintbrush and the diluted glue, paint over the wall. Lay the first sheet of tissue paper on top, allowing it to crinkle. Place more sheets round the first, overlapping the edges. Paint over the tissue paper with diluted glue. Using tweezers, lay the flowers and leaves in a border design on top and smooth gently into place with a small paintbrush. Spray the paints randomly and in fine layers over the whole surface, allowing each colour to dry before applying the next.

MARGUERITE AND CITRUS SHELF EDGING

*M*ake a feature of an ordinary wooden shelf by decorating it with slices of dried lime and large white marguerite flowers. First colourwash the shelf, using paints to match; when dry, apply extra paint with a dry brush. Replace the standard shelf brackets with attractive fretwork brackets, available from hardware stores, and paint them to match.

g a t h e r

dried lime slices
scissors
glue gun
wooden shelf
artificial marguerite flowers

1 Cut the dried lime slices in half with scissors to make half circles that will fit along the edge of the shelf.

2 Working on a protected surface, glue the halved lime slices along the shelf edge, with the cut sides against the top edge of the shelf.

3 Cut the marguerite flowers from the stems and glue at jaunty angles along the shelf edge. Place some on top of the lime slices, poking the stem ends through the flesh of the fruit.

FLORAL CURTAIN TIE-BACK

*T*his minimalist tie-back is quickly made from a piece of scrim ribbon studded with artificial flowers. Use it to hold back a length of plain white muslin, allowing the sun to filter through a bedroom window. Scrim is an ideal fabric to use with flowers – simply poke the stems through its open weave and secure with a few stitches. Daisies are used here, but you can choose any flower that fits in with your decor.

g a t h e r

(FOR EACH TIE-BACK)
wide, pale green scrim ribbon
scissors
sewing needle
sewing threads: pale green and stem green
2 brass rings
artificial daisies

1 Hold the ribbon loosely round the curtain to gauge the length needed for the tie-back. Cut both ends at an angle, turn under and stitch, using matching thread. Stitch a brass ring to the point of each end of the tie-back.

2 Trim the daisy stems to approximately 1 cm (1/2 in). Poke through the scrim from front to back, so that the daisies sit on the surface in a random pattern. Stitch to secure, using matching thread.

56

CHAMOMILE AND LAVENDER PILLOW

*C*hamomile and lavender are both renowned for helping to relieve insomnia, so together they make the perfect pillow for a weary head. The dried flowers are tucked inside two layers of wadding, so that they will not push through the fabric and be uncomfortable. The traditional "Oxford"-style pillowcase is decorated with an artificial white daisy, to match the chamomile flowers inside.

g a t h e r

100 g (4 oz) dried lavender flowers
50 g (2 oz) dried chamomile flowers
10 drops of pure lavender essential oil
10 drops of pure chamomile essential oil
mixing bowl
2 pieces of wadding, 29 x 26 cm (11½ x 10¼ in)
and 30 x 27 cm (12 x 10½ in)
sewing machine
white sewing thread
white cotton fabric, 33 x 30 cm (13 x 12 in)
2 pieces of blue-and-white gingham cotton fabric,
each 41 x 38 cm (16 x 15 in)
dressmaker's pins
large sewing needle
artificial marguerite flower

Mix the lavender and chamomile flowers with the essential oils in a bowl. Cover and leave to steep for one week.

Place the smaller piece of wadding on a flat surface and fold widthways to find the centre. Pile the herb mixture on one half, then fold over the other side to make a sandwich. Machine stitch round all three open sides. Lay the remaining piece of wadding on the wrong side of the white cotton fabric. Lay the wadding sandwich on top, then fold the outer wadding in half and stitch, as before.

Place the two pieces of gingham fabric together, right sides facing. Pin, tack and machine stitch round all four sides, leaving a small opening. Turn right side out and place the herb pillow inside. Slip stitch the opening. Make sure the herb pillow is positioned centrally inside the gingham cover, then pin and then stitch a line of top stitching through the gingham fabric only, just outside the edge of the herb pillow. Stitch the marguerite in the centre of the pillow, taking the needle through all layers to give a quilted effect.

WILD POPPY CURTAINS

*T*hese exuberant curtains are wild in every sense of the word! The dramatic silk flowers are easy to apply, and will quickly and easily transform a set of plain curtains or a dull room. There is a wide range of silk flowers now available from large stores and specialist shops, so you can choose almost any flower and colour you please. The flowers will need to be removed when you come to clean the curtains, but you could replace them with a different set.

g a t h e r

scissors
silk flowers
bodkin or darning needle
plain, lined curtains
sewing needle
sewing threads, to match the flowers and stems

1   Trim the flower stems to 4 cm (1¹/₂ in) long. Using a bodkin or darning needle, pierce a hole through the curtain fabric but not through the lining.

2   Poke each flower stem through the curtain fabric so that the flower sits comfortably on the surface. Using matching thread, stitch through the flower at several points to secure.

3   Turn the curtains inside out. Using matching thread, stitch round each stem on the back of the curtain fabric.

For
GIVING
and
CELEBRATING

HERE'S FLOWERS FOR YOU;

HOT LAVENDER, MINTS, SAVORY, MARJORAM;

THE MARIGOLD, THAT GOES TO BED WI' THE SUN.

(William Shakespeare, 1564-1616)

ABOVE AND LEFT: *Scented oils, papers, inks
and other gifts delight all the senses with their
floral-themed colours and fragrances.*

61

INTRODUCTION

The elusive beauty of fresh flowers is perfectly suited to the transient nature of special occasions. Weddings, St Valentine's Day, anniversaries and birthdays have been celebrated throughout the ages, and all enhanced by floral accompaniments.

No special occasion is complete without flowers. Weddings, christenings and birthdays are all traditionally celebrated with bouquets and floral decorations. Flowers symbolize the cycle of life and the changing seasons. At Harvest Festival, they display the riches of the earth in glowing autumnal shades. Winter brings Christmas, with kissing boughs of mistletoe and glossy holly, bright with berries if the birds haven't got there first! (You can let the birds have their Yuletide feast, to help them through the lean winter, and replace the berries with wired glass ones from a floristry supplier.) Snowdrops make pretty posies for early spring brides, before the whole kaleidoscope of flowers becomes available once more in the summer months.

ABOVE: *A single stem, finished with a matching ribbon, makes a perfect gift any time.*

In a painting of Queen Victoria's birthday party of 1896, the entire room is decked with greenery and the initials "VR" are clearly picked out above the dining table in ivy. It is easy to personalize decorations in the same way, without going to vast expense. Simply train ivy around initials formed from malleable wire to make instant "topiary".

Container plants can be brought inside to add glamour to a party – add white fairy lights to sturdy box plants for a sophisticated entrance. Remember the golden rule, that one flower or plant used in quantity looks much more effective than sparse amounts of a variety of blooms and foliage. Even hedgerow plants such as cow parsley and elderflowers add a celebratory air to a room if used without restraint – fill every container you have and stand

them around the room in groups for added impact. Candles always bring a special, romantic air to any celebration. They flatter your guests and hide less-than-perfect standards of housekeeping, and their warmth brings out the fragrance of the flowers. Match the fragrance of the candles to the species of flower for perfect sensory delight.

Of course, flowers in all their forms make wonderful and very acceptable gifts. There is no need, though, to spend vast sums of money on bouquets and forced arrangements. The

ABOVE: *The flower motifs on the vase and the china plate mirror the delicate shapes of fresh blooms in this informal display.*

fashion these days is for informal flowers, wrapped in natural materials such as brown paper tied with jute twine. Preserved flowers and gifts such as flower-filled sachets and pillows are always welcome, particularly if the scents and colours are chosen to reflect the tastes of the recipient.

BRIDESMAID'S ROSE CIRCLET

*T*his enchanting hair decoration uses dainty rosebuds, so it will be perfectly in scale for even the tiniest bridesmaid. Made of fresh and paper flowers, the circlet is very lightweight to wear; if necessary, you can add hair grips, concealed among the flowers and ribbons. Check the size as you work, and make adjustments so that the design looks good from all angles – keep one side smooth and flat to sit comfortably on the bridesmaid's head. The fresh rosebuds will dry naturally, making the circlet a permanent keepsake of a special day.

g a t h e r

7 deep red and 7 damask pink,
stemmed paper rosebuds, with wired paper leaves
medium-gauge florist's wire
gutta percha tape, to match paper rosebud stems
10 fresh rosebuds, in toning shades
of red and pink
1 m (1 yd) wire-edged pink-and-white
gingham ribbon
- scissors

1   Twist the stems of the red and pink paper rosebuds together to form a circle. Keep all the flowerheads facing in the same direction.

2   Wire and tape the stems of the fresh rosebuds. Attach to the circlet, concealing the joins with tape. Cut the ribbon into three equal lengths and tie in bows. Wire the bows to the circlet, spacing them equally.

SCRAPBOOK CAMELLIA COLLAGE

THOU CANST NOT STIR A FLOWER,
WITHOUT TROUBLING OF A STAR.

(Francis Thompson, 1859-1907)

g a t h e r

old wooden picture frame
brown wrapping paper
silver tissue paper
ultra-high-tack PVA glue
assorted scraps, for example: braid, fringing, safety pins,
needles, embroidery threads, jute twine, letters, etc
dried leaves and petals
cocktail stick
Dutch metal leaf and gilding size or
picture framer's gold paint and brush

Make this very personal gift using small scraps and flowers that will evoke special meaning and memories for the recipient. Take your inspiration from prized possessions, hobbies or interests, or significant places. This collage includes sewing tools, braids and embroidery threads, carefully arranged with some camellia petals which had fallen and dried naturally on a friend's garden path. The underside of the petals is displayed here as the pale, subtle colour beautifully complements the nostalgic theme of this unique gift.

Remove the glass from the frame and cut the brown paper to fit inside. Roughly tear triangular shapes from the silver tissue paper and glue over the frame and onto the brown paper. Glue a border of braid, then build up the rest of the picture. Use the cocktail stick to glue small scraps in place. Highlight the design with the gold leaf or gold paint. Leave to dry, then replace the glass.

ANNIVERSARY PETAL GIFT BOX

Traditionally the first year of marriage is celebrated with paper gifts. Make an entwined heart out of paper string and present it in a heart-shaped box with some rose petal confetti saved from the wedding. The small boxes of herbs also have special significance: rosemary for remembrance, and sage for domestic virtue. You can include other small mementoes as appropriate.

gather

tea towel, with heart motifs
heart-shaped wooden box, with lid
small boxes or jars of dried rosemary and sage
rose petal confetti
sprigs of fresh rosemary
paper string
brown paper luggage label, with string

Fold the tea towel neatly and place in the box. Nestle the boxes or jars of herbs within its folds. Scatter the confetti and rosemary sprigs on top. Unravel the paper string and make a heart shape out of a single strand, twisting it round itself and bending it into shape. Place the string heart in the box, add the lid, then tie more paper string round the box. Write and attach the luggage label, tucking in extra rosemary sprigs to decorate.

67

ROSE BEADS

*I*t is said that the first rosary beads were literally made of roses pounded with essential oils and sweet-smelling resins. This pretty birthday gift borrows from that tradition and mixes the rose beads with silver zodiac charms appropriate to the astrological sign of the recipient. When the beads are worn next to the skin, the warmth of the body will release the delicate rose scent.

g a t h e r

food processor
petals from 12 red roses
approximately 300 ml (¹/₂ pint) rose water
cast iron skillet
12 drops of pure rose essential oil
12 g (¹/₂ oz) gum benzoin powder
12 g (¹/₂ oz) gum acacia powder
kitchen paper
darning needle
wooden cocktail sticks
potato
silver leaf and gilding size or silver acrylic paint
small paintbrush
To make the necklace:
fine black leather cord
silver heart charm and 2 silver zodiac charms
12 black beads, in graduated sizes
4 rose-quartz-coloured glass beads

1 Using a food processor, blend the rose petals and 175 ml (6 fl oz) of rose water until the petals are finely chopped. Simmer the mixture in the skillet for 1 hour, turn off the heat and leave to stand overnight. Add the essential oil and enough rose water to cover. Repeat the simmering and cooling process.

2 Stir in the benzoin and gum acacia. Form the mixture into small beads and place on kitchen paper. When almost dry, pierce the centre of each bead with a darning needle. Leave them to dry on cocktail sticks stuck into a potato. Decorate with traces of silver leaf or paint. Thread all the beads and charms onto the leather cord, alternating them in an attractive design.

PURPLE ALL THE GROUND WITH VERNAL FLOWERS...

THE WHITE-PINK, AND THE PANSY FREAKED WITH JET,

THE GLOWING VIOLET,

THE MUSK-ROSE, AND THE WELL ATTIRED WOODBINE,

WITH COWSLIPS WAN THAT HANG THE PENSIVE HEAD,

AND EVERY FLOWER THAT SAD EMBROIDERY WEARS.

(John Milton, 1608-74)

WALL-MOUNTED FLOWERPOT

*G*ive a common or garden terracotta flowerpot the antique treatment by painting it in subdued colours, using a dry brush to create a patchy, distressed look. Decorate the pot with silk rosebuds and give the finished gift to a non-gardener to brighten up a plain or unattractive wall. Even when summer is over, this flowerpot will still be in full bloom with a gorgeous display of preserved roses. Secure the flowers in florist's dry foam, topped with a layer of moss.

g a t h e r

terracotta flowerpot
paintbrush
acrylic paints: dull green, black,
white and muddy brown
glue gun
silk rosebuds, on wired stems
pliers
protective gloves
wire coathanger

1 Working on a protected surface, paint the outside of the pot with a dry brush, using all the paint colours. Dry brush the inside with muddy brown paint.

2 Glue the rosebuds round the sides of the pot in a random, trailing design. Using pliers and wearing protective gloves, untwist the coathanger and make into a loop to suspend the pot.

FRAMED GERBERA

Gerbera flowers come in such a zingy array of vibrant colours that they merit being framed as works of art. Choose a single bloom and display it upside down in the centre of a piece of watercolour paper, as an unusual and striking gift. Dry brush the picture frame to match the different, toning shades of colour in the petals.

gather

small paintbrushes
acrylic paints, to tone with the gerbera flower
kitchen paper
wooden picture frame, without glass
watercolour paper
scissors
PVA glue
gerbera flower, dried in desiccant

1   Working on a protected surface, load a paintbrush with a small amount of paint. Wipe the excess on a piece of kitchen paper so that just a trace of paint remains. Rub the brush randomly over the frame, following the grain of the wood. Repeat with the other colours. Leave to dry.

2   Cut the watercolour paper to fit inside the picture frame. Using a paintbrush, apply a small amount of glue to the face of the flower.

3   Press the flower firmly but gently in the centre of the watercolour paper, taking care to retain the natural curves of the petals. Leave to dry thoroughly.

SCENTED SPICE KEEPSAKE

$\mathcal{M}$etal biscuit-cutters, rose pot pourri and robust spices are an irresistible combination, making you feel as if you were in a cottage kitchen full of the delicious aroma of home baking. Presented in a wooden frame, they would make a lovely house-warming present. Colourwash the frame with green paint then outline the inner edge with red. Drill small holes in the back of the frame in a simple, folk art heart design, to release the evocative spicy scent.

g a t h e r

rectangular wooden frame, with glass
3 heart-shaped metal biscuit-cutters
dried rosebuds
rose pot pourri
green cardamom pods
pink and black peppercorns
clear adhesive tape

1   Place the wooden frame upside down on a protected surface. Space the biscuit-cutters at equal distances on top of the glass. Surround the cutters with rosebuds, wedging them in place.

2   Fill inside the biscuit-cutters with the rose pot pourri, cardamom pods and peppercorns.

3   Tape over the biscuit-cutters to secure the contents. Add extra pot pourri until the frame is full.

4   Replace the back of the frame.

74

TUSSY MUSSY

*F*ull of fresh herbs and flowers, tussy mussies were carried in the 16th century to ward off illness and disguise unpleasant smells. Use the language of flowers to create a personalized tussy mussy for a special gift. The glorious damask rose used here is Rosa mundi, which symbolizes variety. Sweet peas are included for their intoxicating fragrance, and also for their message of "delicate pleasures". The softly frilled edging of lady's mantle leaves makes a symbolically protective circle round the posy.

g a t h e r

large damask rose
7 sweet pea flower stems
9 leaves and 5 flowerheads of lady's
mantle (Alchemilla mollis)
florist's tape

A SENSITIVE PLANT IN A
GARDEN GREW,
AND THE YOUNG WINDS FED IT
WITH SILVER DEW.
(P.B. Shelley, 1792-1822)

Hold the rose in one hand and gradually surround it with the lady's mantle flowers, then the sweet peas, adding them with your other hand. Turn the posy as you work to form a neat circle. Finally add the lady's mantle leaves. Bind the stems together with florist's tape.

TRACERY OF LEAVES GIFT WRAP

This cool green arrangement of pressed leaves, caught beneath translucent paper, makes elegant wrapping paper for a special gift. Use transparent adhesive tape to join the paper when you make up a parcel. For a man, tie the parcel with jute twine; for a woman, use pale green silk or satin ribbon.

g a t h e r

spray adhesive
pale green speckled paper
pressed elder leaves
tracing paper
heavy books

Spray evenly over the surface of the paper with adhesive. Lay the leaves on top in a random design, taking care not to crease them. Spray the leaves with adhesive. Place the tracing paper on top and weigh down with heavy books overnight.

PRESSED FLOWER GIFT TAG

$\mathcal{G}$ive ordinary brown paper designer status with the simple addition of a few pressed flowers. Make the gift tag to fit neatly into the envelope, sealed with a scrap of flower petal. For a co-ordinated gift, wrap a pot plant in a brown paper bag sprinkled with the same flowers – pansies, roses, primulas and geraniums all press well and can be grown in pots.

g a t h e r

scrap card

brown paper

scissors

small brown envelope

small paintbrush

PVA glue

pressed flowers

scalpel

1 Working on a piece of scrap card, cut a gift tag out of the brown paper so that it fits the envelope when folded in half. Score along the fold line with the scissors.

2 Using a small paintbrush, apply a tiny amount of glue to the faces of the flowers, holding each flower steady as you work.

4 Working on a piece of scrap card, and using a scalpel, carefully remove the overlapping edges of the petals.

5 Glue one of the petal offcuts onto the envelope flap, so that it overlaps the edge. Write the gift tag, then put it in the envelope and glue the rest of the petal offcut onto the envelope to seal.

3 Press the flowers onto the gift tag, so that they overlap the edges of the tag. Leave to dry.

FLORAL GREETINGS CARD

*C*onventional pressed flower pictures and greetings cards often crowd together masses of material, creating a cluttered effect. For a fresh look at this craft, restrict your design to a single pressed flower and make the most of its shape. Try placing the undersides of the petals uppermost for a change – the soft colours are a gentle reflection of the stronger colours on the upper surface of the petals, which seems appropriate to the ethereal, nostalgic quality of preserved flowers. This flower is the lovely Delft blue *Osteospermum*.

g a t h e r

watercolour paper
scissors
envelope
gilding size
small paintbrushes
sheet of gold leaf or Dutch metal leaf, plus gilding size
PVA glue
pressed flower
tweezers

1   Working on a protected surface, cut the watercolour paper to fit the envelope when folded in half. Using a paintbrush, apply gilding size to selected areas at two opposite corners of the card front. Leave for about 15 minutes (or following the manufacturer's instructions), until tacky. Press the gold or metal leaf onto the size.

2   Using a clean paintbrush, apply glue sparingly to the face of the flower. Pick the flower up with tweezers and gently lay face down on the card front. Press lightly to secure.

FLOWER-SCENTED INK

*F*loral-scented ink adds a wonderfully romantic touch to letters. A perfect gift for any age would be a labelled bottle of ink with matching scented writing paper. Choose an essential oil and flowers to suit the colour of the ink, for example lavender oil with violet-coloured ink. Strong-coloured inks and strong fragrances are best for this purpose, as adding alcohol will dilute them both slightly.

g a t h e r

(TO MAKE 1 BOTTLE OF INK)

25 drops of essential oil, to match ink colour
1 ml (1/8 teaspoon) vodka
small ceramic bowl or saucer
funnel
empty essential oil bottle
14 ml (1/2 fl oz) bottle of coloured ink
copper plant tag
used ballpoint pen
short length of raffia or narrow silk ribbon
dried or fresh flowers

1 Mix the essential oil and vodka together in the bowl or saucer. Decant into the empty essential oil bottle. Stand the bottle of ink in the bowl to catch any drips, then add the oil mixture a drop at a time.

2 Inscribe the name of the scent or flower on the copper tag, using an old ballpoint pen. Tie the tag round the neck of the ink bottle with raffia or ribbon, and decorate with flowers.

TRAPPED-FLOWER STATIONERY

*T*his personalized notepaper is created by trapping pressed flowers under a layer of tissue paper, giving the brightly coloured petals a soft, nostalgic look. Decorate envelopes to match, using a pressed flower to seal each flap. To present a set of this stationery as a gift, place it in a box with a fragranced sachet – be careful to keep the sachet from touching the paper, otherwise the oils may stain it.

gather

matching notepaper and envelopes
spray adhesive
pressed pansies
tissue paper
scissors

Spray the notepaper with adhesive and arrange the pressed pansies on the glued surface. Spray again lightly then lay the tissue paper on top, allowing it to form attractive crinkles and creases. Leave to dry then trim the excess tissue paper. For the envelope flaps, decorate a piece of notepaper in the same way but leave the tissue paper hanging over the edge. Cut the notepaper to size and glue it to the envelope flap. Tuck the excess tissue paper inside the envelope and glue in place.

83

LINEN FLOWER FRAGRANCER

Modern synthetically perfumed fabric conditioners have their uses, but for old-fashioned luxury and comfort nothing can beat the delicate fragrance of real flowers to scent your bedlinen and underwear. Choose flowers and essential oil to match the floral motif embroidered on a handkerchief, and pack them in a pretty tissue-lined box. To use, sprinkle a few drops on the handkerchief and add to your tumble drier or linen cupboard.

gather

small shallow box, with lid
tissue paper, in 2 colours to tone with the embroidery
scissors
white card, on string or thread
small bottle of pure essential oil, to match the embroidered flowers
embroidered handkerchief, with flower motif
fresh flowers and petals

1 Line the box with the tissue paper, cutting it to fit. Offset the paper to reveal both colours.

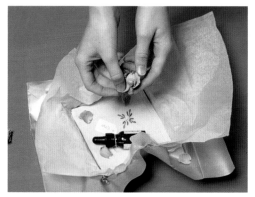

2 Write directions for use on the white card and tie it round the neck of the essential oil bottle. Lay the embroidered handkerchief in the box and nestle the bottle on top. Scatter fresh flowers and petals in the folds of the handkerchief.

84

ROSE PETAL CONFETTI

What could be more romantic than real rose petal confetti? Dry the petals naturally on baking sheets in your airing cupboard or by the side of a stove, turning them intermittently so that they dry evenly. Present the confetti in pretty little tulle bags, to be distributed among the guests by the bridesmaids.

gather

marker pen
side plate
paper
clear adhesive tape
scraps of white tulle
scissors
dessertspoon
air-dried fragrant rose petals
organdie ribbon

Using a marker pen, draw round a side plate onto a piece of paper to make a template. Tape scraps of tulle on top and cut out. Lay two tulle circles on top of each other and place a dessertspoonful of dried petals in the centre. Draw up both layers together to make a small bag, and tie a ribbon bow round the neck.

85

For
PAMPERING
and
FRAGRANCING

AND I WILL MAKE THEE BEDS OF ROSES,

AND A THOUSAND FRAGRANT POESIES.

(Christopher Marlowe, 1564-93)

ABOVE AND LEFT: *Flower-scented oils and lotions are the ultimate in indulgent luxury.*

87

INTRODUCTION

Flowers have an incomparable beneficial effect on mind, body and spirit alike; in turn soothing and reviving. They delight the senses at every turn, whether as fresh petals scattered in a simple infusion, or as fabulously evocative essential oils in a therapeutic bath.

Floral oils, lotions, powders and waters have been used to perfume the body and the home for centuries. The Greeks made fragrant oils from roses, thyme, lilies, sage, marjoram, anise root and orris root – the root of the flag iris, a violet-scented rhizome which is also a floral fixative. Orris root is used in many pot pourri mixes even today. In Elizabethan times, strings of orris root were placed in the final rinsing water of fine linens to imbue them with a lasting floral fragrance.

For many years, and in many societies, bathing was considered dangerous to both body and soul. Instead, oils scented with flowers and herbs were used to cleanse and anoint the body as far back as 1000 BC. The introduction of

ABOVE: *The beneficial effects of flowers have long been used in pomanders and sachets.*

baths was viewed with much suspicion, and bathing was undertaken only occasionally, say, monthly. Nobility were usually the first to introduce new trends. Elizabeth I used washballs blended from flowers and imported Castile soap, and had a powder mixed especially for her which she would apply after her bath. It consisted of ground spices, orris root and rose petals, a blend which would be equally appealing today.

Despite these attempts at cleanliness, there have been many times in history when surroundings as well as individuals have needed the help of fragrances to cloak the unpleasant odours resulting from poor sanitation, unhygienic food practices and disease. The Elizabethans used strewing herbs as a kind of disposable

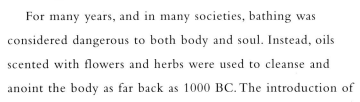

ABOVE: *Elderflower cordial makes a refreshing drink.*

carpet; Elizabeth I's favourite strewing herb was meadowsweet, and bergamot, woodruff and rosemary were also popular. We know now that many flowers and herbs have anti-bacterial powers, although it would have taken more than carrying a tussy mussy or pomander to ward off the plague or smallpox. Cardinal Wolsey carried a clove-studded pomander with him on his pastoral visits to fend off the odour emanating from his less savoury parishioners. Even if it did nothing for his health, it must certainly have made life more pleasant.

The sybaritic pleasures afforded by floral preparations have enduring appeal. The finest perfumes in the world require vast quantities of fresh flowers to produce the essential oils on which they are based. It takes an acre of roses to yield only 4½ kg (10 lb) of attar of roses, hence the high price of pure essential oils and blended perfumes. Eau de colognes are a more affordable alternative, since the basic perfume is diluted to make it go further. Since the 19th century, manufacturers have guarded their secret recipes and have fought to gain the rights to produce the definitive eau de cologne. Hardly surprising, when such important characters as Napoleon used several bottles a day.

The idea of making a floral perfume into a personal trademark is not a new one. Napoleon and Josephine adored violets, and Josephine and her successor for Napoleon's love, Marie-Louise, both used violets as their signature scent; Marie-Louise established production of the Parma violet and the making of violet water. Nell Gwynne, mistress of Charles II, adored lavender water, the most popular fragrance of the Stuart period, and Madame de Pompadour and Marie Antoinette both used vast quantities of scented vinegars and eau de colognes daily.

BELOW: *An acre of roses yields just 4½ kg (10 lb) of attar of roses.*

Our reasons for using floral distillations today may be rather different to our ancestors, but we also need to pamper ourselves with beautiful fragrances. The modern world is often so hectic that it is a luxury to relax, surrounded by the soothing and restoring scents of herbs and flowers.

TOILE DE JOUY NIGHTDRESS CASE

Toile de Jouy combines elegance with rustic simplicity, making it the perfect partner for a simple butter muslin sachet of soporific lavender flowers. For a more potent fragrance, an additional, larger sachet of flowers could be placed between the layers of lining fabric and wadding. This idea could also be adapted to make a wonderful quilted hot water bottle cover, with the heat of the water bottle intensifying the lavender aroma.

g a t h e r

blue cotton toile de Jouy fabric, 50 cm (20 in) square

scissors

fabric motifs

pins and sewing needle

tacking thread and matching threads

piece of natural wadding, 50 cm (20 in) square

piece of tracing paper, 50 cm (20 in) square

cream cotton lining fabric, 50 cm (20 in) square

2 pieces of natural-coloured butter muslin,

10 cm (4 in) square

12 g (½ oz) dried lavender flowerheads

10 cm (4 in) miniature blue ribbon

1 m (1 yd) of 1 cm (½ in) tricolour silk ribbon

Cut out three panels of toile de Jouy fabric, each measuring 30 x 21 cm (12 x 8¼ in), centring the fabric motifs on each panel. Cut one of the panels to a triangular point or whatever shape mirrors the central motif. Pin, tack and stitch the toile panels together so that the motifs are the right way up on what will be the flap, the face and the back of the nightdress case. Trim the wadding, tracing paper and lining fabric to the same size and shape as the face of the nightdress case. Place the pieced toile and the fabric right sides together, then place the wadding and tracing paper on top of the lining.

Pin, tack and stitch around the perimeter of the case, leaving a small gap for turning. Turn the case right side out and slip stitch the gap closed. Fold up the front panel and slip stitch the sides together to form the case.

To make the sachet, pull threads from the muslin in a grid pattern. Cut out two heart shapes from the muslin. Pin, tack and stitch together, leaving a small gap. Fill with lavender, then continue stitching to close the gap. Trim the heart sachet with the miniature blue ribbon. Make a simple bow from the tricolour ribbon, and stitch the lavender sachet and ribbon bow in place on the nightdress case.

SUMMER FIELDS DRAWER LINERS

Shop-bought drawer liners are very popular but this version is altogether superior. The soft, absorbent texture of watercolour paper makes it ideal for this purpose, and it is readily available from art suppliers in large single sheets which you can cut to fit the drawer. The scents of lemon grass, cedar and rosewood appeal to men and women alike, and an added advantage is that the mixture will deter moths.

g a t h e r

25 g (1 oz) gum benzoin powder
50 g (2 oz) ground orris root
25 drops each of pure essential oils: lemon grass, cedar and rosewood
10 drops of pure orange essential oil
ceramic mixing bowl
wooden spoon
2 pieces of wadding, the same size as the cut watercolour paper
scissors
needle or sewing machine
matching sewing threads
2 pieces of lightweight cotton fabric, the same size as the wadding plus 1.5 cm (5/8 in) seam allowance
dressmaker's pins
embroidery needle and embroidery thread
large sheet of watercolour paper or blotting paper
large cellophane bag
jute twine
ears of wheat

Mix the benzoin powder, orris root and essential oils together in a bowl. Cover and leave to steep for one week.

Hand or machine stitch the two pieces of wadding together, sandwiching the scented mixture between the two layers. Right sides facing, place the two pieces of cotton fabric together. Pin, tack and stitch, leaving a small opening. Turn right side out and insert the scented wadding. Slip stitch the opening.

Using the embroidery needle and embroidery thread, make a few knotted tufts at regular intervals to hold the wadding evenly in place. Place the scented fabric sachet on the watercolour or blotting paper. Roll up the paper with the sachet inside. Place in the cellophane bag and seal tightly. Leave for 2 weeks. Remove the paper from the bag and re-roll. Tie with twine and decorate with the ears of wheat.

ROSE AND NEROLI POT POURRI

Make this traditional Victorian recipe using the most fragrant petals you can find, picked *à point* – at the peak of perfection. Include petals which have a sentimental significance, for example, roses given by a loved one or flowers from a wedding bouquet. Scented with a potent mixture of essential oils and spices, this pot pourri will keep for a decade in a closed container. The dried roses used to decorate the container have been coated in 1 tablespoon of sunflower oil scented with 4 drops of pure rose essential oil and left to steep in a sealed container.

1 Remove the rose petals and place on the kitchen paper, to remove any moisture.

gather

12 fragrant fresh red or pink roses
kitchen paper
glass jar, with lid
100 g (4 oz) sea salt
small lid or saucer, to fit inside glass jar
wooden spoon
12 g (½ oz) whole allspice
25 g (1 oz) whole cinnamon
1 teaspoon ground cloves
mortar and pestle
sealed container
25 ml (1 fl oz) rose water
10 drops of pure rose essential oil
7 drops of pure rose geranium essential oil
7 drops of pure neroli essential oil
50 g (2 oz) lavender flowers
12 g (½ oz) ground orris root
12 g (½ oz) ground mace
12 g (½ oz) pink peppercorns
1 teaspoon ground nutmeg
decorative ceramic container, with lid

2 Place a layer of petals in the glass jar and sprinkle with some of the sea salt. Build up more layers in the same way. Weigh down, then put the lid on the jar. Leave for 10 days in a cool, dry place, stirring each day with a wooden spoon. Pour off any liquid.

3 Grind the spices in the mortar and reserve half in a sealed container. Remove the petals from the jar and re-layer with the spices. Replace the lid and leave for 3 weeks. Stir in the rose water, oils, lavender, spices and reserved spices. Leave for 2 weeks, then transfer to the ceramic container.

SEASHORE LAVENDER POT POURRI

This unusual version of pot pourri is also an evocative display of natural materials, a constant reminder of childhood holidays by the sea. The scent and colour of the lavender conjure up vivid images of lavender fields near a dramatic sea coast. Sea salt absorbs essential oil beautifully and the resulting effect recalls glistening sands at low tide. Only the border of the plate will be visible, so choose one with a decorative edge.

gather

450 g (1 lb) dried lavender flowers
large, flat plate with blue-and-white border
225 g (8 oz) coarse sea salt
3 dried lotus root slices
3 ears of wheat
dried starfish
12 drops of pure lavender essential oil
kitchen foil

1   Lay a generous layer of dried lavender flowers in two parallel lines along each side of the plate, keeping a space roughly the same width as each layer of lavender between them.

2   Fill the space between the lavender with sea salt. Sprinkle a trickle of sea salt along the outside edges of the lavender.

3   Break the lotus root slices in half and tuck them under the outside edges of the lavender. Lay the ears of wheat across the sea salt. Add the dried starfish in the centre.

4   Drip the lavender oil onto the lavender and lotus root slices. Cover the plate with kitchen foil and leave the pot pourri to steep for 2 weeks.

ROSE-SCENTED COATHANGER

Padded fabric coathangers always add a note of elegance to your wardrobe, all the more so when the filling is sweetly scented pot pourri. Make your own pot pourri mixture, using pure rose essential oil for a fragrance that will lift your spirits every time you open the wardrobe door. To cover the coathanger, choose a deep pink floral-patterned fabric, such as this beautiful toile de Jouy print.

gather

wooden coathanger, with screw-in hook
2 pieces of deep pink toile de Jouy fabric, each 25 cm (10 in) x 1½ times the length of the coathanger
sewing machine
matching sewing threads
scissors
rose-scented pot pourri
sewing needle
1 m (1 yd) deep pink, narrow silk ribbon

1   Unscrew the hook from the coathanger. Place the two pieces of toile de Jouy fabric right sides together and machine stitch with matching sewing threads along three sides, leaving one short side open. Turn the cover right side out and slip it over the coathanger. Fill with rose-scented pot pourri.

2   Slip stitch the open end of the cover to close. Stitch a row of running stitch along the top, just above the coathanger, then gather the fabric to fit the coathanger.

3   Screw the hook back in place, fitting it through the seam. Wind the ribbon round the hook and secure with tiny stitches, using toning thread. Tie a ribbon bow round the neck of the coathanger.

NO-SEW WARDROBE SACHETS

Beautifully worked lace-edged handkerchiefs and dressing table mats sadly have
little use today, but you can give them a new
lease of life by filling them with herbs and
spices to deter moths and scent your wardrobe.
The mixture used here is spicy and fresh-
smelling, so it will equally appeal to the male
members of the household. The quantities
given are enough to fill 12 sachets.

g a t h e r

100 g (4 oz) dried leaves
4 cinnamon sticks
25 g (1 oz) whole cloves
25 g (1 oz) whole orris root
25 g (1 oz) whole peppercorns
mortar and pestle
ceramic bowl
approximately 10 drops of pure lavender essential oil
approximately 10 drops of pure rose essential oil
kitchen foil
metal spoon
lace-edged handkerchiefs and dressing table mats
jute twine
small posies of fresh or dried flowers,
with wired and taped stems
grey satin ribbon

1 Crumble the dried leaves into small
pieces with your fingers.

2 Crush all the spices with the mortar
and pestle. Put them into a ceramic
bowl and drop by drop add the essential oils
until you achieve a pleasant scent. Blend well,
cover with kitchen foil and leave for 24 hours.

3 Mix the spices with the dried leaves.
Cover with foil and leave the mixture
for at least 2 weeks.

4   Place a spoonful of the mixture in the
centre of a mat or handkerchief. Draw
up the corners and then the sides.

5   Tie the jute twine tightly round the
neck of the sachet.

6   Tie a posy of flowers round the neck
of the sachet, using the ribbon.

TUDOR FLOWER WASHBALLS

*T*hese pretty little balls of soap are perfumed in the traditional way with floral oils. Use different oils to suit your personality or skin type, for example, grapefruit oil to wake you up in the morning. The flower petals can also be added at the mixing stage, so that they are dispersed throughout the soap and act as a gentle exfoliant.

gather

cheese grater
large bar of pure, unperfumed soap
heatproof mixing bowl, jug of boiling water
disposable plastic gloves
5 drops of pure lavender essential oil
4 drops of pure rose essential oil
3 drops of pure chamomile essential oil
fresh rose petals or lavender flowers

Grate the soap into the bowl. Gradually add a small amount of boiling water until the mixture forms a very stiff paste – use mineral water or spring water for best results. Wearing plastic gloves, mix in the essential oils. Take small handfuls of the soap and oil mixture and form into balls. Press the rose petals or lavender into the surface while the washballs are still moist. Leave to dry thoroughly.

WRAPPED AND SCENTED SOAP

*P*erfume a simple bar of soap with scented silk ribbon for old-fashioned bathtime luxury. Trimmed with flowers to match, it will add a touch of luxury to your bathroom shelf. The cool grey-blue of lavender is an elegant choice. You could also use pure rose essential oil, teamed with pink ribbon and dried rosebuds, or neroli oil with orange ribbon and pieces of dried orange peel.

gather

(FOR EACH BAR OF UNPERFUMED SOAP)
8 drops of pure lavender essential oil
pale lavender silk or rayon ribbon
covered container
sprigs of dried lavender

Drip the essential oil onto the ribbon and leave in a covered container for two weeks. Wrap a length of the scented ribbon round each bar of soap and knot securely, tucking sprigs of lavender into the bow.

INFUSED FLOWER OIL

The fragrance of this oil is not as intense as the pure essential oils, but it is an excellent way to make the most of an abundance of highly scented flowers in your garden. Use lavender or roses, such as the fabulous Rosa mundi, a variety as stunning today as when it was introduced over 300 years ago. Pick the flowers *à point*, and dry them on kitchen paper. Repeat the infusing process with more petals until the oil is sufficiently perfumed; if you run out of petals, you can add a little pure essential oil to intensify the fragrance.

g a t h e r

fragrant flowers
sterile glass jar, with stopper
cold-pressed sunflower oil
sieve

1   Remove the petals from the flowers and pack as many as possible into the sterile glass jar.

2   Pour over enough oil to cover the petals and replace the stopper. Leave the jar outside in the sun for a few weeks, bringing it indoors at night. Strain through a sieve and discard the flowers.

ELDERFLOWER SKIN TONIC

A splash of this skin tonic, applied straight from the refrigerator, will instantly transport you to the cool green depths of the summer countryside. Make it up according to your skin type, using natural ingredients that are well known for their beneficial effects: cider vinegar for normal skin, witch hazel for slightly oily or troubled skin, or vodka for excessively oily skin and open pores. The tonic will remain fresh in the refrigerator for several days, or you can freeze it for later use. For presentation, decant into a sterilized glass bottle with a decorative stopper.

g a t h e r

10 elderflower heads
heatproof mixing bowl
300 ml (¹/₂ pint) still bottled water
saucepan
1 tablespoon cider vinegar, witch hazel or vodka
clean tea towel
ladle
sieve
sterilized glass jar, with lid

WHERE'ER YOU TREAD, THE

BLUSHING FLOWERS SHALL RISE.

(Alexander Pope, 1688-1744)

2   Boil the bottled water in a saucepan and pour over the flowers. Cover with a tea towel and leave for 20 minutes. Add the cider vinegar, witch hazel or vodka, cover and leave overnight to infuse.

3   Ladle the fluid through a sieve into the sterilized jar, cover and leave to cool. Store in the refrigerator.

1   Strip the flowerheads from the stems and place in the heatproof bowl.

CALMING MILK BATH MIXTURE

*C*hamomile and neroli both have many valuable properties, essentially to soothe and calm. Chamomile is a wonderfully gentle herb, used to settle upset stomachs and to treat insomnia; it is also used in beauty preparations to pacify sensitive skin. Neroli oil comes from the flowers of the Seville orange tree and is known to relieve depression, anxiety and insomnia. Add this soothing mixture to a running bath and allow a traditional remedy to soak away the cares of everyday life. For a gift, present the mixture in a decorated bag accompanied by a bottle of the matching oils.

g a t h e r

120 ml / 4 fl oz / 1/2 cup fine sea salt
240 ml / 8 fl oz / 1 cup powdered milk
6 drops of pure chamomile essential oil
12 drops of pure neroli essential oil
ceramic mixing bowl
covered container
small calico drawstring bag
dried chamomile or strawflower flowerheads
dried orange slice
fresh flowers
grosgrain ribbon
extra chamomile and neroli essential oils
funnel
empty essential oil bottle
scrim ribbon
embroidery thread, to match scrim ribbon

Mix the sea salt, powdered milk and essential oils well. Place in a covered container and leave for 3 weeks. Decant into the calico bag, adding a few dried flowerheads. Decorate the bag with the dried orange slice, fresh flowers and grosgrain ribbon. Mix extra essential oils in the same proportions and use to fill the empty bottle. Write instructions for use on a piece of scrim ribbon and tie round the neck of the bottle, using embroidery thread.

MARIGOLD INFUSION

g a t h e r

heatproof bowl
20 marigold flowerheads
metal spoon
tea towel
sieve
funnel
sterilized bottle, with stopper

Golden marigold flowers have long been used by country people as first aid treatment for cuts, grazes and stings. Apply this refreshing infusion as a skin lotion, or on a cold compress to ease the pain of sprained or over-exerted muscles. Many other flowers can be made into therapeutic infusions – chamomile, lavender, eyebright, elder, yarrow and meadowsweet are good choices. Gather the flowers at their peak to maximize the soothing properties of the infusion. You will need approximately 1 teaspoonful of dried flowers or 3 teaspoonfuls of fresh flowers to each cup of water. Use mineral water or fresh spring water for the best results.

Warm the bowl with hot water. Place the flowerheads and metal spoon in the bowl and pour over 4 cups of just-boiled water. (The spoon will prevent the bowl from cracking.) Cover with a tea towel and leave to stand for 10 minutes. Strain the clear liquid through a sieve into the bottle.

ROSE POMANDER

ost rose pomanders are made with tightly furled rosebuds but this glorious adaptation uses the large, open blooms of dried Gerdo roses, with their beautiful rhubarb-and-custard colouring. Fragranced with neroli and rose essential oils, it is quick and easy to make. This pomander is too fragile to crowd into a wardrobe, so display it from a bedpost or dressing table mirror. Carried by a bridesmaid, it would make a lovely alternative to a posy of fresh flowers. Match the colours of the ribbons to the shades of the roses.

g a t h e r

dried roses, on stems
florist's scissors
florist's dry foam
florist's wire
glue gun
60 cm (24 in) of 1.5 cm (⅝ in) wide grosgrain ribbon
1 m (1 yd) of 5 cm (2 in) wide wire-edged ribbon
a few drops of pure neroli and rose essential oils

1 Trim the rose stems to about 2 cm (¾ in). Cut a round ball of florist's dry foam and poke the stems into it, packing the rose heads tightly together.

2 Add more roses, working in even bands towards the top and bottom of the ball of foam. Leave a small area at the top for attaching the hanger.

3 Working on a protected surface, make a loop of florist's wire and poke both ends into the space at the top of the ball. Glue firmly in place.

4 Wrap the wire loop with the grosgrain ribbon. Secure each end with a spot of glue. Tie a bow round the loop, using the wire-edged ribbon. Add the neroli and rose essential oils to complete.

For
ENTERTAINING
and
FEASTING

THE BUD MAY HAVE A BITTER TASTE,
BUT SWEET WILL BE THE FLOWER.

(William Cowper, 1731-1800)

ABOVE AND LEFT: *A luscious feast of summer fruits is set off with a simple, yet dramatic natural display.*

INTRODUCTION

Flowers add a theatrical flourish to the simplest of dishes and transform any mealtime into an occasion. With their colour, fragrance, and delicate flavours, they enhance rather than overwhelm whatever they accompany.

Using flowers in cooking as well as for decoration is an ancient tradition, dating back thousands of years. In Eastern European, Indian and Middle Eastern cuisine, the delicate flavours and scents of orange blossom and rose petals are very popular. These flowers, and waters infused with their fragrance, appear in many recipes throughout the world. Both sweet and savoury dishes benefit from their subtle touch – Turkish delight, baklava (Greek syrup-soaked pastries) and kheer (Indian creamed rice, flavoured with cardamom and rose water, and decorated with silver leaf) are just a few of the more well-known recipes. Flower waters are also used widely to flavour ice creams, sorbets, jams and jellies, blancmanges and salad dressings.

Floral cordials and syrups are more intensely perfumed, and can be simply made at home from any highly scented

ABOVE: *Edible flowers are an attractive and exotic ingredient.*

edible blossom. Honeysuckle, violets, clove-scented pinks, primroses, orange blossom, lilac, freesias, elderflowers and lavender all taste delicious. Just a spoonful gives an extra lift to salad dressings, marinades and barbecue sauces, as well as their more familiar use in desserts. In winter, add a spoonful of floral syrup to a tisane for a warming, calming drink, or to hot mulled wine or cider for a potent medieval mid-winter drink.

To make a simple floral syrup, choose flowers that have not been chemically treated and pick them at the peak of fragrance. Remove the bitter white heel from the base of each petal before using. Place 225 g (½ lb) of petals (a single variety or a mixture of sympathetic flowers) in a saucepan and add 300 ml (½ pint) of water to cover. Bring to the boil, cover with a lid and leave to steep for 30 minutes. Strain and return to the pan with 175 g

ABOVE: *Floral ice cubes make a pretty, lightly flavoured addition to drinks.*

ABOVE: *Nasturtiums and pansies have a peppery bite. You should avoid eating pansy flowers in the first three months of pregnancy.*

(6 oz) sugar. Simmer for 10 minutes then strain the syrup into a sterilized bottle.

Flowers themselves are, of course, a rich source of inspiration in cookery. Courgette flowers, stuffed with a rich, herby filling of mixed Italian cheeses and fried in a light batter until pale golden, have long been a Mediterranean delicacy. Nasturtiums add a peppery bite to salads, and other flowers are used more for their colour than their flavour or perfume. Marigolds, cornflowers, pansies, geraniums, gladioli and day lilies add little in the way of taste, but look so delightful that the palate is stimulated by their beauty alone. Float a single, stunning day lily on a tureen of chilled soup for an elegant conversation piece, or drop a few heads of brilliant blue borage into a jug of lemonade for a cooling summer drink.

Floral sugar adds a subtle extra ingredient to cakes and biscuits. Finely grind edible, fragrant, dried petals and mix 1 part flowers to 4 parts caster sugar. Place in a covered container and leave to infuse for a month or so before using.

113

SPICED ROSEBUD NAPKIN RINGS

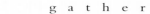

Turn an ordinary meal into an occasion with crisp damask napkins trimmed with spicily scented flowers and herbs. These simple bundles of cinnamon sticks, rosemary sprigs and fresh rosebuds are very quick and easy to assemble, but they look and smell delicious. Your guests can take the napkin decorations home, where they will dry out naturally and remain fragrant.

gather

(FOR EACH NAPKIN RING)
sprig of fresh rosemary
cinnamon stick
2-3 small fresh rosebuds, with stems
5 cm (2 in) narrow, heavy-duty, green florist's tape
60 cm (24 in) narrow, pale green satin ribbon

1 Lay a sprig of rosemary along the curved edge of each cinnamon stick.

2 Remove excess leaves from the rosebud stems. Lay on top of the rosemary at the centre of the cinnamon stick. Wrap the florist's tape securely round the bundle to hold all the elements together.

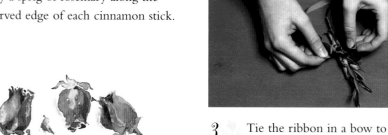

3 Tie the ribbon in a bow to conceal the tape, leaving the ends long to tie round the napkin.

IVY-DRAPED CANDLE SCONCE

This baroque decoration for a simple candle sconce takes only moments to prepare, yet creates a very romantic setting to welcome your guests. Gather long pieces of wild ivy and simply wind them through and round the metal sconce – they will naturally twine and curve into attractive shapes. Do not let the candles burn down as far as the foliage, and remember never to leave them unattended.

g a t h e r

florist's scissors
ivy
metal candle sconce
12 dried yellow roses
3 paper hellebores (Christmas roses), on wired stems

1 Trim any dying or decayed leaves from the ivy. Wind each piece through and round the candle sconce, allowing the metal to show through.

2 Trim the dried rose stems to 2.5 cm (1 in) and poke into the ivy framework. Trim the wired paper rose stems to 7 cm (2¾ in) and entwine through the ivy. Arrange the ivy leaves to cover the joins.

DOUBLE NASTURTIUM SALAD

*T*his colourful summer salad is a feast for the eyes as well as the tastebuds. It is well-known that black pepper enhances the flavour of strawberries; here, vinegar and oil infused with raspberries and strawberries return the compliment by adding a sweet note to peppery nasturtiums. You can prepare the dressing ahead, but do not make the salad until immediately before serving.

g a t h e r

(SERVES 4)

D r e s s i n g

small bowl

whisk

sea salt

1 tablespoon raspberry vinegar

¹/₂ tablespoon balsamic vinegar

1 teaspoon honey

2 tablespoons olive oil, infused with

orange and lemon peel

2¹/₂ tablespoons groundnut oil, infused with strawberries

freshly ground black pepper

S a l a d

orange pepper, seeded

cherry tomatoes

mixed salad leaves, for example, frisée,

radicchio and red oak leaf

double nasturtium flowers and leaves

large, flat serving plate

lemon slices

To make the dressing, whisk together the salt and vinegars. Blend in the honey. Slowly whisk in the oils until thoroughly blended. Add black pepper to taste.

Slice the pepper and cut the tomatoes in half. Wash the salad and nasturtium leaves, but not the flowers. Tear the salad leaves and place on the plate with the nasturtium leaves. Toss lightly in the dressing. Add the pepper and tomatoes. At the last minute, add the nasturtium flowers and lemon slices.

118

ELDERFLOWER CHAMPAGNE

This beautifully fragrant, bubbly drink has a wonderfully celebratory air. It conjures up images of rural wedding parties in the 19th century, with trestle tables spread in the shade of the orchard. It is not real champagne, but certainly you should not underestimate its potency. Winemaking can often seem rather a daunting business, requiring specialist equipment, but this recipe is simplicity itself. It will make sufficient to see you through a whole summer of parties and special events.

gather

12 elderflower heads
large sterilized bowl or bucket
juice and zest of 1 lemon
2 tablespoons white wine vinegar
700 g (1¹/₂ lb) caster sugar
muslin
funnel
sterilized bottles and corks

Strip the elderflower heads from the stalks. Place the flowers in the bowl or bucket together with the lemon juice. Add the vinegar, sugar, lemon zest and 4.5 litres (1 gallon) of water. Cover the bowl or bucket with a piece of muslin and leave for 24 hours. Strain the mixture through a fresh piece of muslin into the sterilized bottles. Cork the bottles. Leave for 2 weeks before drinking.

FLORAL ICE BOWL

1 Clip or tape the bowls together. Pour water between the two bowls until the level rises to halfway.

2 Place the flowers between the two bowls, pushing some of the stems below the inner bowl so that the flowers cannot rise to the top during freezing. Poke extra individual flowerheads through the framework of leaves. Pour in water to within 1 cm (1/2 in) of the top of the bowls. Freeze. Turn both bowls upside down and place under gently running cold water for a few seconds to release the ice bowl.

An ice bowl is a spectacular centrepiece at a summer party and will last long enough for your guests to enjoy a chilled dessert. Ice bowls were very popular in grand Victorian houses, when pineapples and other exotic fruit were brought in from the greenhouse. Choose the flowers to complement the colours of the dessert – these are the brightly coloured *Geum* "Mrs Bradshaw". You can tape two bowls one inside the other but a set of clip-together ice bowls, available from good kitchen suppliers, will save you the trouble. Decorate the rim of the ice bowl with more fresh flowers and leaves just before you carry it to the table.

g a t h e r

*set of clip-together ice bowls or two bowls held
together with heavy-duty florist's tape
large jug
12 brightly coloured flowers, with leaves
and stems attached*

SWEET FLOWERS ALONE CAN SAY
WHAT PASSION FEARS REVEALING.

(Thomas Hood, 1799-1845)

LAVENDER AND THYME BUTTER

Fresh lavender and thyme flowers, picked from the herb garden, impart a delightfully subtle and intriguing flavour to unsalted butter. Serve with delicate jams and jellies, or with savoury sandwich fillings — an open sandwich of roast chicken on crusty bread spread with this piquant herb butter is a lovely picnic treat. For real flowery flavour, serve with fresh rose petals.

g a t h e r

250 g (9 oz) unsalted butter
muslin
30 fresh lavender spikes
10 fresh thyme sprigs
small bowl, with lid

Wrap the unsalted butter in the muslin. Place half the mixed lavender and thyme in the bowl and then lay the wrapped butter on the bed of flowers. Pack more flowers round the butter. Cover the bowl and leave in the refrigerator overnight for the butter to absorb the flavours.

LEFT: *This sandwich of rose petals and lavender and thyme butter is best enjoyed out of doors, on a balmy summer evening.*

EDIBLE FLOWERS ON A FROSTED ORANGE CAKE

*E*dible flowers make an exquisite decoration for a special-occasion cake. Dipped individually in orange flower water and sugar, their delicate scent complements the citrus tang of this homemade orange cake perfectly. Choose small, pretty flowers such as violets or pansies. Extra crystallized flowers will keep well, stored in a tin; the cake itself will no doubt disappear very quickly!

CRYSTALLIZED FLOWERS
g a t h e r

300 ml (¹/2 pint) orange-flower water
small saucepan
whisk
60 g (2¹/2 oz) edible gum arabic
tweezers
edible flowers
100 g (4 oz) caster sugar
kitchen paper
wire cooling rack
airtight tin

1   Warm the orange-flower water in the saucepan. Whisk in the gum arabic and allow to cool.

2   Using tweezers, dip each flower in the mixture. Shake to remove the excess. Dip each flower in the sugar. Place on kitchen paper on a wire rack to dry. Store in an airtight tin lined with kitchen paper.

ORANGE CAKE
g a t h e r

250 g (9 oz) unsalted butter, softened
250 g (9 oz) caster sugar
electric mixer
4 large eggs
250 g (9 oz) self-raising flour, sifted
grated zest of 1 orange
2 cake tins, 20 cm (8 in) round and 4 cm (1¹/2 in) deep

Preheat the oven to 190°C/375°F/Gas 5. Place the butter and caster sugar in the mixing bowl and beat on high speed until very light and fluffy. Add one egg and beat for several minutes. Continue adding the other eggs, one at a time. Add the flour all at once. Add the orange zest and mix in well.

Butter and flour the cake tins. Divide the cake mixture between them. Bake in a preheated oven for 30 minutes, or until the cakes spring back when lightly touched in the centre. Cool on the wire rack in the tins for 5 minutes, then remove the cakes from the tins and leave on the rack to cool completely.

ORANGE FROSTING

g a t h e r

75 g (3 oz) unsalted butter, softened
400 g (14 oz) icing sugar, sifted
juice of 1 orange
mixing bowl

Place the butter, icing sugar and half the orange juice in the bowl. Beat well, adding more orange juice as necessary to make the frosting smooth and spreadable. Sandwich the cakes together with the frosting, then cover the top and sides with the remaining frosting.

INDEX

INDEX

PICTURE ACKNOWLEDGEMENTS

The publishers are grateful to the following for pictures published in this book: Bridgeman Art Library: p10 Indian miniature from the Basohli kingdom; p11 *Echo and Narcissus* by John Waterhouse; p12 *Madonna di Ognissanti* by Ambrogio Giotto; Visual Arts Library: p8 Egyptian painting; p9 *The Bridesmaids* ; p12 *La Primavera* (fresco); p13 *The Lady and the Rose* by Eduard Niczky; p14 *The Roman Window* by Dante Gabriel Rossetti, Museo de Arts de Ponce, Ganesh with garland; p15 Victorian greeting card; ET Archive: p8 *The Aged Mullah* (Mogul miniature); p10 *The Tree of Life* (mosaic from Basilica Aquileia); p13 *Primavera* by Sandro Botticelli.

ACKNOWLEDGEMENTS

A book such as this inevitably involves a cast, if not of thousands, then certainly of more people than one might imagine. I would like to thank Mavis Davis and Bev at Swindon Wholesale Flowers, who were unerringly enthusiastic, knowledgeable and helpful, for supplying fresh, dried and artificial flowers, preserved fruit slices and foliage, miniature terracotta pots and sundries such as florist's foam, wire and gutta percha tape for use throughout. Mary and Daisy at The Natural Fabric Company supplied the cream fabric for the wild poppy curtains, blue toile for the nightdress case, red toile for the coathangers, natural lining fabrics, butter muslin for scented sachets and milk jug cover, natural wadding and feather cushion pads throughout. Michelle Kershaw and Cath Stobbart at Lakeland Plastics Ltd were their usual efficient and friendly selves and organized the mail order supply of the linen scrims for the gerbera cushion, the artificial flowers for the wild poppy curtains, and the ice bowl maker. Annabel Lewis of V V Rouleaux supplied the subtle rayon ribbons for the wrapped soap. The Dollshouse Draper kindly sent the irresistibly delicate silk ribbons for the tracery of leaves gift wrap, rose-scented coathanger, and many other projects in the book. Wedding Belles of Marlborough supplied the charming bridesmaid's dress for the bridesmaid's rose circlet, and a tulle veil as a background for photography throughout. Many basic materials were kindly supplied by the following companies as follows: spray adhesives from 3M; hot melt glue guns and glue from Bostik; emulsion paints from Crown

Expressions; varnishes from Cuprinol; PVA adhesive from Unibond; staple gun and staples from Black and Decker; dried lavender heads from Jersey Lavender; water-based wood dyes from Liberon; pencils from Berol; additional plants from Country Gardens; and the decorative shelf supports for the citrus and marguerite shelf edging from Jali.

Pat and Chris Cutforth opened their home and garden to us and allowed us to cut some of their beautiful flowers for photography, such as the Geum "Mrs Bradshaw" in the ice bowl, the Rosa mundi in the infused oil, and great swathes of elderflower and other blooms and foliage for use in the photography. Pat also baked the citrus cake for me to decorate. Mrs Hicks endured us trampling through her usually well-ordered domain and remained good-humoured despite the havoc we wreaked, while a special mention must go to David Smith, who tends Mr and Mrs Cutforth's garden with such expert care and so supplied us with such a riot of glorious blooms to choose from.

My husband Andrew and daughter Daisy are always involved in the creation of my books, whether helping me gather materials, tolerating missed meals and erratic housekeeping, or joining me in research trips to obscure museums, libraries and plant collections on what we jokingly term our family holidays.

Last, but definitely not least, I would like to thank my mother for teaching me how to make poppy ballerinas, fuchsia fairies and other natural creations during the seemingly endless summers of my childhood in our Norfolk garden.